W9-BVR-189

FOCUS ON THE FAMILY® PRESENTS

Your Child™

VIDEO SEMINAR

essentials of DISCIPLINE

What's OK, What's Not and What Works

with Dr. James Dobson
adapted by Steve and Anne Wamberg

Participant's Guide

Tyndale House Publishers, Inc.
Carol Stream, Illinois

Your Child Video Seminar: Essentials of Discipline, Participant's Guide

A Focus on the Family book published by Tyndale House Publishers, Carol Stream, Illinois.

Focus on the Family and the accompanying logo and design are federally registered trademarks of Focus on the Family, Colorado Springs, CO 80995.

TYNDALE and Tyndale's quill logo are registered trademarks of Tyndale House Publishers Inc.

Scripture quotations are from the HOLY BIBLE, NEW INTERNATIONAL VERSION ®. Copyright © 1973, 1978, 1984 by the International Bible Society. Used by permission of Zondervan. All rights reserved.

Excerpts from the following used by permission:

The Complete Marriage and Family Home Reference Guide by Dr. James Dobson, © 2000 by James Dobson, Inc. Published by Tyndale House Publishers, Inc., Carol Stream, Illinois. All rights reserved.

The New Dare to Discipline by Dr. James Dobson, © 1970, 1992 by James C. Dobson. Published by Tyndale House Publishers, Inc., Carol Stream, Illinois. All rights reserved.

The Strong-Willed Child by Dr. James Dobson, © 1978 by James Dobson. Published by Tyndale House Publishers, Inc., Carol Stream, Illinois. All rights reserved.

The New Strong-Willed Child by Dr. James Dobson, © 2004 by James Dobson, Inc. Published by Tyndale House Publishers, Inc., Carol Stream, Illinois. All rights reserved.

Parenting Isn't for Cowards by Dr. James Dobson, © 1987 by James C. Dobson. Published by Word Publishing, Dallas, Texas. All rights reserved.

Bringing up Boys by Dr. James Dobson, © 2001 by James Dobson, Inc. Published by Tyndale House Publishers, Inc., Carol Stream, Illinois. All rights reserved.

Editors: John Duckworth & Mick Silva
Cover design: Peak Creative
Interior design: Angela Messinger
Interior artwork: Cornerstone Media

ISBN-13: 978-1-58997-189-9
ISBN-10: 1-58997-189-2

Printed in the United States of America
8 9 / 10

TABLE OF CONTENTS

DISCIPLINE, PART 1

DISCIPLINE, PART 2

THE STRONG-WILLED CHILD

Welcome!

If there's anything a busy parent like you doesn't need, it's one more thing to do.

Unless, of course, that one thing might make the *other* things a whole lot easier.

We can't guarantee that taking part in this course will squeeze all the stress out of being a mom or dad. It won't change the diapers, make your kids wolf down asparagus, or dial down the volume on your teenager's CD player.

But it *will* help you to take the stresses in stride. That's because you'll learn how to be a calmer, more confident parent—one who exercises healthy leadership at home, helps your child develop self-discipline and respect for authority, and expresses unconditional love in ways your child can see and feel.

In other words, you'll discover how to be the kind of parent you really want to be.

That takes a little effort, but it doesn't take boredom or busy work.

So we've designed this course to be practical and fun. At its heart is an entertaining, down-to-earth video series featuring popular author, broadcaster, experienced parent, and psychologist Dr. James Dobson. And in your hands is the book that's going to make it all personal for you—the participant's guide.

In each chapter of this book, you'll find the following sections:

VI   YOUR CHILD VIDEO SEMINAR

- *HOME BASE* Here's where you get started—with some intriguing thoughts from Dr. Dobson.
- *YOUR STORY* Try these interactive exercises to figure out where you stand on the subject at hand.
- *SCREEN TIME* Use this section to help you take notes as you watch the video.
- *WORDWORKS* This brief Bible study has all you'll need, including thought-provoking questions and the Scripture passages themselves—so you won't have to look them up.
- *YOUR WAY* Here's where the rubber meets the road. The creative tools in this section help you come up with your own action plan—applying the principles you've learned to your one-of-a-kind family.
- *TECH SUPPORT* Got questions? Dr. Dobson has answers to get you through the week.

Whether you're using this book as part of a group or on your own, taking a few minutes to read and complete each chapter will bring the messages of the video home.

And isn't that exactly where you and your child need it most?

CHAPTER 1

WHY YOUR CHILD
NEEDS DISCIPLINE

HOME BASE
getting started

I boarded a plane, found my seat, and glanced to my left. Seated across from me this time was a well-dressed woman and a *very* ambitious two-year-old girl. Correction! The mother was seated but her daughter was most definitely not. This little girl had no intention of sitting down—or slowing down. It was also obvious that the mother did not have control of the child, and indeed, Superman himself might have had difficulty harnessing her. . . .

In a few minutes, the flight attendant came by and urged the mother to buckle the child down. Easy for her to say! I will never forget what occurred in the next few minutes. The two-year-old threw a tantrum that must have set some kind of international record for violence

and expended energy. She was kicking, sobbing, screaming, and writhing for freedom! Twice she tore loose from
her mom's arms and scurried toward the aisle. The morti-
fied woman was literally begging her child to settle down
and cooperate. Everyone in our section of the plane was
embarrassed for the humiliated mother. Those of us
within ten feet were also virtually deaf by that point.

Finally, the plane taxied down the runway and took
off with the mother hanging onto this thrashing toddler
with all her strength. Once we were airborne, she was
able at last to release the little fireball. When the crisis
was over, the mother covered her face with both hands
and wept. I felt her pain too.

Why didn't I help her? Because my advice would
have offended the mother. The child desperately needed
the security of strong parental leadership at that
moment, but the woman had no idea how to provide it.

—Dr. James Dobson in *Parenting Isn't for Cowards*

YOUR STORY
*discovering where
you stand*

1. If your family were the subject of a TV show,
which of the following might be the title?

____ *Little House on the Prairie*

____ *Little Kids on the Floor*

____ *Little Rest for the Weary*

____ *Little Spank on the Bottom*

____ *Little Angels in the Outfield*

____ *Little Rascals on Parole*

2. If your approach to disciplining your child(ren)
were a TV show, which of the following would best
describe it?

___ *Monday Night Football*
___ *Tuesday Night Tantrums*
___ *Wednesday Night Wimpiness*
___ *Thursday Night Threats*
___ *Friday Night Frustration*
___ *Saturday Night Serenity*

3. Which of these TV show titles describes the way discipline was handled in your home when you were growing up?
___ *Father Knows Best*
___ *Father Knows Belts*
___ *Father Knows Brats*
___ *Father Knows Nothing*
___ *Father's Not the Boss*
___ *Father's Not Around*

4. If having "control of the TV remote" means having the authority in your family, who in your family most often seems to "control the remote"? Why?

5. Let's say you work for *TV Guide* writing short summaries of episode plots. Write a summary of how disciplining your child(ren) went this week in your home.

6. When it comes to discipline, which parts of the last week do you wish could be "edited out"? Why?

7. Where do you need the most help from a "director" in the way you discipline your child(ren)?

8. What kind of "happy ending" do you hope results from disciplining your child(ren)?

SCREEN TIME
discussing the video

1. If you were parenting "expert" Dr. O'Blivious in the video, what would you do about his kids' behavior?
___ Exactly what he did—nothing
___ Try to reason with them
___ Cry
___ Yell until they listen to me
___ Spank them when I got them home
___ Admit defeat
___ (other) _____

2. Discipline isn't something you do to a child; it's something you do . . .

3. One way to show our kids we love them is to . . .

4. It's important to balance . . .

5. A child without love will . . .

6. Parental leadership is a . . .

WORDWORKS
*input from
the Bible*

1. "Blessed is the man you discipline, O LORD; the man you teach from your law; you grant him relief from days of trouble, till a pit is dug for the wicked" (Psalm 94:12-13).

Do you think of discipline as a "blessing"? Why or why not?

Do your kids think of discipline as a good thing? Have you ever tried to get them to see it that way? If so, what happened?

How could discipline grant someone "relief from days of trouble"? Has that ever happened for you?

How could discipline spare your child(ren) trouble in the future?

2. "The proverbs of Solomon son of David, king of Israel:
> for attaining wisdom and discipline;
>> for understanding words of insight;
> for acquiring a disciplined and prudent life,
>> doing what is right and just and fair;
> for giving prudence to the simple,
>> knowledge and discretion to the young—
> let the wise listen and add to their learning,
>> and let the discerning get guidance—
> for understanding proverbs and parables,
>> the sayings and riddles of the wise.
> The fear of the LORD is the beginning of knowledge,
>> but fools despise wisdom and discipline"
>>> (Proverbs 1:1-7).

Discipline is tied to a whole shopping list of favorable character traits in this passage. Which three would you most like to see in your child(ren)?

This passage says that "the fear [an awed respect] of the LORD is the beginning of knowledge." If a child doesn't have this respect for God, how does it make the job of disciplining harder for a parent? Do you feel your children have this foundation? How can you tell?

Take a look at that "shopping list" again. Do you see your child(ren) making progress in any of those areas? If so, how might your discipline have helped?

3. "Love the LORD your God and keep his requirements, his decrees, his laws and his commands always. Remember today that your children were not the ones who saw and experienced the discipline of the LORD your God: his majesty, his mighty hand, his outstretched arm" (Deuteronomy 11:1-2).

When you read about "the discipline of the LORD," what feelings and images come to your mind?

What would you like your child(ren) to feel and think when they hear a phrase like "the discipline of the LORD"?

What do you think your role should be in telling your child(ren) about God's discipline?

YOUR WAY
applying the principles

1. What scares you most about discipline?

2. What scares you least after watching the video?

3. Which of the following do you need most to work on this week?

____ Seeing myself as an authority figure

____ Being more consistent in the way I discipline my child(ren)

____ Seeing discipline as an expression of love

____ Setting boundaries for my child(ren)

____ (other) _____

4. How will you try to teach your child(ren) to respect your authority this week? Complete one of the following sentences to summarize your plan. Here's an

example: "I'll work on my tendency to back down when my son argues with me about doing his homework."
- I'll draw the line when it comes to . . .
- I'll work on my tendency to . . .
- I'll read the Bible passage about . . .
- I'll explain to my kids that I . . .
- I'll ask for support from . . .

5. How will you create an atmosphere of *loving* leadership in your home this week? Pick one of the following items and tell how you'll use it to remind your kids that you love them. An example: "I'll set my alarm clock half an hour early on Thursday, so that I can make my daughter's favorite pancakes before she goes to school."

A meal	A party
The washing machine	The family vehicle
A Bible	A toy
An alarm clock	The TV set

Your plan:

6. If you're parenting with your spouse, complete the following sentences and share them with him or her.
- You could help our child(ren) see me as an authority in our home by . . .

- When it comes to disciplining our child(ren), I most need your support . . .

- When my leadership with our child(ren) seems unloving, you can let me know that by . . .

Q. You don't have to convince me that my kids need discipline. It's obvious! My question is, when are they going to realize that resistance is futile and act the way I want them to?

A. Even if you implement a flawless system of discipline at home, which no one in history has done, your children will be children. At times they will be silly, destructive, lazy, selfish, and—yes—disrespectful. Such is the nature of humanity. We as adults have the same problems. Furthermore, when it comes to kids, that's the way it *should* be. Boys and girls are like clocks; you have to let them run. My point is that the principles in this book are not designed to produce perfect little robots who can sit with their hands folded in the parlor thinking patriotic and noble thoughts! Even if we *could* pull that off, it wouldn't be wise to try.

The objective, as I see it, is to take the raw material with which our babies arrive on this earth, and then gradually mold it into mature, responsible, and God-fearing adults. It is a twenty-year process that will bring progress, setbacks, successes, and failures. When the child turns thirteen, you'll swear for a time that he's missed everything you thought you had taught . . . manners, kindness, grace, and style. But then, maturity begins to take over and the little green shoots from former plantings start to emerge. It is one of the richest experiences in living to watch that progression from infancy to adulthood in the span of two dynamic decades.

—From *The New Dare to Discipline*

Q. I want my child to learn *self*-discipline and *self*-reliance. How does your approach to *external* discipline by parents get translated into internal control?

A. You've asked a provocative question, but one that reveals a misunderstanding of children, I believe. There are many authorities who suggest that parents not discipline their children for the reason implied by your question: they want their kids to discipline themselves. But since young people lack the maturity to generate that self-control, they stumble through childhood without experiencing *either* internal or external discipline. Thus, they enter adult life never having completed an unpleasant assignment, or accepted an order that they disliked, or yielded to the leadership of their elders. Can we expect such a person to exercise self-discipline in young adulthood? I think not. He doesn't even know the meaning of the word.

My concept is that parents should introduce their child to discipline and self-control by the use of external influences when he is young. By being required to behave responsibly, he gains valuable experience in controlling his *own* impulses and resources. Then as he grows into the teen years, the transfer of responsibility is made year by year from the shoulders of the parent directly to the child. He is no longer forced to do what he has learned during earlier years. To illustrate, a child should be *required* to keep his room relatively neat when he is young. Then somewhere during the midteens, his own self-discipline should take over and provide the motivation to continue the task. If it does not, the parent should close his door and let him live in a dump, if necessary.

—From *The Strong-Willed Child*

Q. I'm confused about the difference between *discipline* and *punishment*. Can you clarify it for me?

A. William Glasser, the father of Reality Therapy, made this distinction very clear when he described the difference between discipline and punishment. "Discipline" is directed at the objectionable behavior, and the child will accept its consequence without resentment. He defined "punishment" as a response that is directed at the individual. It represents the desire of one person to hurt another; and it is expression of hostility rather than corrective love. As such, it is often deeply resented by the child.

Although I sometimes use these terms interchangeably, I agree with Glasser's basic premise. Unquestionably, there is a wrong way to correct a child that can make him or her feel unloved, unwanted, and insecure. One of the best guarantees against this happening is a loving conclusion to a disciplinary encounter.

—From *The New Dare to Discipline*

CHAPTER 2

IRRESPONSIBILITY
VS. DEFIANCE

HOME BASE
getting started

I once dealt with a mother of a rebellious thirteen-year-old boy who snubbed every hint of parental authority. He would not come home until at least two o'clock in the morning, and deliberately disobeyed every request she made of him. Assuming that her lack of control was a long-standing difficulty, I asked if she could tell me the history of this problem. She clearly remembered when it all started: Her son was less than three at the time. She carried him to his room and placed him in his crib, and he spit in her face.

She explained the importance of not spitting in mommy's face, but was interrupted by another moist missile. This mother had been told that all confrontations could be resolved by love, understanding, and discussion. So she wiped her face and began again, at which point she was hit with another well-aimed blast. Growing increasingly frustrated, she shook him . . . but not hard enough to disrupt his aim with the next wad.

What could she do then? Her philosophy offered no honorable solution to this embarrassing challenge. Finally, she rushed from the room in utter exasperation, and her little conqueror spat on the back of the door as it shut. She lost; he won! This exasperated mother told me she never had the upper hand with her child after that night!

When parents lose these early confrontations, the later conflicts become harder to win. Parents who are too weak or tired or busy to win make a costly mistake that will haunt them during their child's adolescence. If you can't make a five-year-old pick up his toys, it is unlikely you will exercise much control during his most defiant time of life.

—Dr. James Dobson in *The New Dare to Discipline*

YOUR STORY
discovering where you stand

How can you avoid the heartbreak experienced by the mother of that spitting three-year-old? Should you punish everything that looks like misbehavior? Can you ever afford to back down from a confrontation? Before looking for answers, let's find out how you and your family are doing in this area. Check the responses that best reflect your feelings and opinions.

1. Sometimes I feel like my kids are out of control.
____ Strongly agree
____ Somewhat agree
____ Don't know
____ Somewhat disagree
____ Strongly disagree

2. You should start disciplining children when they're 18 months old.

___ Strongly agree

___ Somewhat agree

___ Don't know

___ Somewhat disagree

___ Strongly disagree

3. My kids never question my authority.

___ Strongly agree

___ Somewhat agree

___ Don't know

___ Somewhat disagree

___ Strongly disagree

4. Children should be punished for making a mess.

___ Strongly agree

___ Somewhat agree

___ Don't know

___ Somewhat disagree

___ Strongly disagree

5. If my toddler had a tantrum in public, I would know what to do.

___ Strongly agree

___ Somewhat agree

___ Don't know

___ Somewhat disagree

___ Strongly disagree

6. It's usually best to ignore it when kids misbehave.

___ Strongly agree

____ Somewhat agree

____ Don't know

____ Somewhat disagree

____ Strongly disagree

7. Teenagers are too old to be disciplined.

____ Strongly agree

____ Somewhat agree

____ Don't know

____ Somewhat disagree

____ Strongly disagree

8. I wish I'd confronted my children's disobedience when they were younger.

____ Strongly agree

____ Somewhat agree

____ Don't know

____ Somewhat disagree

____ Strongly disagree

9. My parents disciplined me too much, and I don't want to repeat that mistake.

____ Strongly agree

____ Somewhat agree

____ Don't know

____ Somewhat disagree

____ Strongly disagree

10. Requiring your children to obey will hurt them in the long run.

____ Strongly agree

____ Somewhat agree

___ Don't know
___ Somewhat disagree
___ Strongly disagree

In the space that follows, describe (or draw) a time when your child crossed a "line in the sand" that you'd drawn—that is, when he or she ignored a boundary you'd set. Maybe it was a warning to be in bed by a certain time, or to stop playing with food at the table. How did you react? If you could do it over again, would you respond differently? Why or why not?

SCREEN TIME
discussing the video

1. The supermarket scene: What would you do?

___ Pray that the floor would open and swallow me up
___ Pretend he was somebody else's kid
___ Ignore the behavior
___ Spank him in the store
___ Spank him in the parking lot
___ (other) _____

2. According to Dr. Dobson, childish irresponsibility looks like . . .

3. Willful defiance looks like . . .

4. It's important to meet the challenge to your authority because . . .

5. The ultimate paradox of parenthood is that children want . . .

6. The six principles of earning the right to lead your child are:

a. Define boundaries in advance
b. Respond with confident decisiveness
c. Distinguish between childhood irresponsibility vs. defiance
d. Reassure & teach after confrontation
e. Avoid impossible demands
f. Let love be your guide

WORDWORKS
input from the Bible

1. "At the end of your life you will groan, when your flesh and body are spent. You will say, 'How I hated discipline! How my heart spurned correction! I would not obey my teachers or listen to my instructors. I have come to the brink of utter ruin in the midst of the whole assembly'" (Proverbs 5:11-14).

What three words might describe the feelings of this person who's looking back on his or her life?

What does that tell you about the value of discipline?

2. "The evil deeds of a wicked man ensnare him; the cords of his sin hold him fast. He will die for lack of discipline, led astray by his own great folly" (Proverbs 5:22-23).

"He who ignores discipline comes to poverty and shame, but whoever heeds correction is honored" (Proverbs 13:18).

"Discipline your son, for in that there is hope; do not be a willing party to his death" (Proverbs 19:18).

According to these verses, what can eventually happen to a child who hasn't been disciplined?

What kinds of "death" could a lack of discipline lead to?

3. "A fool spurns his father's discipline, but whoever heeds correction shows prudence" (Proverbs 15:5).

Children have a choice of whether to spurn or heed discipline. How can a parent show that it's better to heed than to spurn?

4. "Folly is bound up in the heart of a child, but the rod of discipline will drive it far from him" (Proverbs 22:15).

How does this verse contrast with the view that children are a "blank slate" at birth, and that they'll do the right thing unless parents teach them otherwise?

According to this verse, what might happen if a parent doesn't deal with a child's challenges to his or her authority?

5. "No discipline seems pleasant at the time, but painful. Later on, however, it produces a harvest of righteousness and peace for those who have been trained by it" (Hebrews 12:11).

How could this verse help a parent with the stress of having to confront a defiant child?

YOUR WAY
applying the principles

1. How have you been dealing with childish irresponsibility and willful defiance? Can you tell the difference? Take a look at the following "crimes" and draw lines to match them with the "punishments" that would be typical in your home. (Feel free to use some penalties more than once, and others not at all.) Be ready to explain your choices.

Crime	Punishment
Accidentally spilling milk	Going to jail
Staying out two hours past curfew	$1 fine
Misplacing eyeglasses for the first time	None
Misplacing eyeglasses after being warned	Being grounded
Refusing to do homework	Spanking
Breaking sister's leg in a fight	Loss of TV for a week
Selling drugs	$20 fine
Telling you to "shut up"	A long talk
Accidentally breaking your favorite dish	Time out

2. In the first column below, write the names of your children. Now think back over the last month, especially the times when your children behaved in ways you wish they hadn't. How much of this behavior do you think was

childish irresponsibility (carelessness due to lack of maturity), and how much was willful defiance (challenging your
authority as a parent)? For each child, write a percentage
representing each category.

Child's Name:
Childish Irresponsibility:
Willful Defiance:

Child's Name:
Childish Irresponsibility:
Willful Defiance:

Child's Name:
Childish Irresponsibility:
Willful Defiance:

Based on these percentages, which of the following do
you think is true?

____ I've been spending too much time punishing care-
       lessness.
____ I haven't been spending enough time confronting
       defiance.
____ I've been spending about the right amount of
       time dealing with both.
____ Other:

If you have more than one child, what do these percentages tell you about how you need to deal differently
with each one?

If your spouse is studying this topic with you, compare answers with him or her. Do the two of you tend to put the same behavior in different categories? How might this encourage you to "punish" a mistake—or ignore a challenge to your authority?

3. When it comes to "drawing a line in the sand," which of the following areas do you need to work on? Check all that apply.

___ Choosing my battles more carefully

___ Knowing where to draw the line

___ Not backing down when I've drawn a line

___ Administering the right penalty when the line is crossed

___ Administering penalties in a loving way

4. Think of a boundary you need to establish this week for one of your children—a line you need to draw in the sand. Maybe it's a bedtime, bath time, room cleaning standard, or a ban on name-calling. To make the boundary as clear as possible, try writing it in ten words or less.

Now decide how you'll enforce that boundary if it's crossed. Describe the penalty in ten words or less.

What will be hardest for you about following through on setting and enforcing this boundary? In the following space, write a prayer request about that. If possible, share that request with someone else.

Q. My child just started the "terrible twos." It seems like she does nothing *but* challenge my authority. How many times do I have to enforce the boundaries before she gives up?

A. Moms and dads should not hope to make their two-year-olds act like more mature children. A controlling but patient hand will eventually succeed in settling the little anarchist, but probably not until he is between three and four. Unfortunately, however, the child's attitude toward authority can be severely damaged during his toddler years. Parents who love their cute little butterball so much that they cannot risk antagonizing him may lose and never regain his control. This is the time to establish themselves, gently but persistently, as the bosses to be reckoned with.

—From *The New Dare to Discipline*

Q. My four-year-old seems to "cross the line" a hundred times a day, causing one mess after another. Maybe it's just childish irresponsibility, but it's driving me nuts. What can I do?

A. Toddlers most often get in trouble for simply exploring and investigating their world. That is a great mistake. Preschoolers learn by poking their fingers into things that adults think they should leave alone. But this busy exploration is extremely important to intellectual stimulation. . . .

I am not suggesting that your child be allowed to destroy your home and all of its contents. Neither is it right to expect her to keep her hands to herself. Parents should remove those items that are fragile or dangerous, and then strew the child's path with fascinating objects of all types. Permit her to explore everything possible, and do not ever punish her for touching something that she did not know was off-limits, regardless of its value. With respect to dangerous items, such as electric plugs and stoves, as well as a few untouchable objects, such as the knobs on the television set, it is possible and necessary to teach and enforce the command "Don't touch!" If the child refuses to obey even after you have made your expectations clear, a mild slap on the hands while saying no will usually discourage repeat episodes.

I would, however, recommend patience and tolerance for all those other everyday episodes that involve neither defiance nor safety.

—From *The Complete Marriage and Family Home Reference Guide*

Q. What about me? I have a teenager, and slapping her on the hand or giving her a "time out" doesn't cut it anymore. What should I do when she's willfully defiant?

A. Discipline for adolescents and teens should involve lost privileges, financial deprivation, and related forms of non-physical retribution. Be creative!

My mother, I might note, was a master of trench warfare during my own stubborn adolescent years. My father was a full-time minister and frequently on the road, so Mom had the primary responsibility for raising me. I was giving my teachers a hard time during this era, and on several occasions was sent to the principal's office, where I received stern lectures and a few swats with an infamous rubber hose (which was permissible back then). This discipline did not change my bad attitude, however, and my mother became increasingly frustrated with my irresponsibility and dropping grades. It wasn't long before she reached her limit.

One day after school she sat me down and said firmly, "I know you have been fooling around in school and ignoring your assignments. I also know you've been getting in trouble with your teachers. . . . Well, I've thought it over, and I've decided that I'm not going to do anything about what is going on. I'm not going to punish you. I'm not going to take away privileges. I'm not even going to talk about it anymore."

I was about to smile in relief when she said, "I do want you to understand one thing, however. If the principal ever calls *me* about your behavior, I promise you that the next day I'm going to school with you. I'm going to walk two feet behind you all day. I will hold your hand in front of all your friends in the hall and at lunch, and I'm going to enter into your conversations throughout the whole day. When you sit in your seat, I'm going to pull my chair alongside you, or I'll even climb into the seat with you. For one full day, I will not be away from your side."

That promise absolutely terrified me. It would have been social suicide to have my "mommy" following me around in front of my friends. No punishment would have been worse! I'm sure my teachers wondered why there was such a sudden improvement in my behavior and a remarkable jump in my grades near the end of my freshman year in high school.

—From *The New Dare to Discipline*

CHAPTER 3

ANGER VS. ACTION

HOME BASE
getting started

There is no more ineffective method of controlling human beings (of all ages) than the use of irritation and anger. . . .

Consider your *own* motivational system. Suppose you are driving your automobile home from work this evening, and you exceed the speed limit by forty miles per hour. Standing on the street corner is a lone policeman who has not been given the means to arrest you. He has no squad car or motorcycle; he wears no badge, carries no gun, and can write no tickets. All he is commissioned to do is stand on the curb and scream insults as you speed past. Would you slow down just because he shakes his fist in protest? Of course not! You might wave to him as you streak by. His anger would achieve little except to make him appear comical and foolish.

On the other hand, nothing influences the way Mr. Motorist drives more than occasionally seeing a black and white vehicle in hot pursuit with nineteen red lights flashing in the rear view mirror. When his car is brought to a stop, a dignified, courteous patrolman approaches the driver's window. He is six foot nine, has a voice like the Lone Ranger, and carries a sawed-off shotgun on each hip. "Sir," he says firmly but politely, "our radar unit indicates you were traveling sixty-five miles per hour in a twenty-five-mile zone. May I see your driver's license, please?" He opens his leatherbound book of citations and leans toward you. He has revealed no hostility and offers no criticisms, yet you immediately go to pieces. You fumble nervously to locate the small document in your wallet (the one with the horrible Polaroid picture). Why are your hands moist and your mouth dry? Why is your heart thumping in your throat? Because the course of *action* that John Law is about to take is notoriously unpleasant. Alas, it is his *action* which dramatically affects your future driving habits.

Disciplinary action influences behavior; anger does not.

—Dr. James Dobson in *The Strong-Willed Child*

YOUR STORY
discovering where you stand

1. Think back over the last week. When it comes to disciplining your child(ren), do you think you were most effective when you . . .

___ waited until you were angry before you took action?

___ took action before you got mad?

___ paid no attention to whether you were angry or not?

___ ignored disobedience and hid in the closet?

2. Did your kids respond best to your discipline when you . . .

__ were angry?

__ were calm?

__ talked to them before you took action?

__ surprised them with your action?

3. On the blank "face" below, draw the expression you tend to have when you discipline your child(ren).

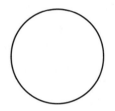

What message do you think that expression sends to your child(ren)?

4. Now draw the face you'd like to have when disciplining.

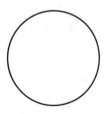

What message would you want that expression to send?

5. In an average day, how much of the time you spend with your child(ren) is spent feeling angry?

___ All the time

___ Most of the time

___ About half the time

___ A quarter of the time

___ Very little

___ None

6. In the space below, draw or write two things your children do that tend to make you angry.

SCREEN TIME
discussing the video

1. According to Dr. Dobson, the most common discipline error parents make is . . .

2. If our kids wait for us to get angry to obey, we're teaching them . . .

3. Effective discipline shows children that with disobedience comes . . .

4. You don't need anger to control children, you need . . .

5. It doesn't take much action to avoid conflict if . . .

WORDWORKS
input from the Bible

1. "O LORD, do not rebuke me in your anger or discipline me in your wrath" (Psalm 6:1).

In this verse, David—a man known for his close relationship with God—prays that God wouldn't discipline him in anger. Why do you suppose he prayed that way?

Did your parents ever discipline you in anger? Did the anger help or hurt?

2. "My dear brothers, take note of this: Everyone should be quick to listen, slow to speak and slow to become angry, for man's anger does not bring about the righteous life that God desires" (James 1:19, 20).

Can a parent who follows this advice be effective in disciplining his or her children? Why or why not?

This verse implies that our anger doesn't accomplish God's purposes. In your experience, does being angry at your kids help to "keep them in line"? Why or why not?

Why might it be wise to keep your anger under control as you discipline a child?

3. "A gentle answer turns away wrath, but a harsh word stirs up anger." (Proverbs 15:1)

Do you think your child(ren) would describe your discipline as gentle or harsh? How would you describe it?

What role does anger usually play in your approach to discipline? Are you satisfied with that?

4. "Those whom I love I rebuke and discipline. So be earnest, and repent" (Revelation 3:19).

Jesus is speaking in this verse. How would you describe His motivation for discipline?

What seems to be His goal?

To "repent" means to be sincerely sorry and to change your behavior accordingly. Does adding anger to discipline make it more likely that a child will repent, or less likely? Why?

Your Way
applying the principles

1. What do you think is the difference between anger and discipline?

2. When you make threats, what percentage of the time do you make good on them? Show your answer by marking an "X" on the following scale.

The Follow-Through-O-Meter

100%	75%	50%	25%	0%

Now mark a "Z" where you'd *like* your answer to be.

3. Think about your "commands" to your kids. Do you expect them to obey? Write or draw in the box what you honestly expect to happen when you ask your child to clean his or her room.

Based on what you just drew or wrote, which of the following do you need to do this week?

___ Nothing

___ Have a higher expectation of my child and hold him or her accountable

___ Lower my expectations

___ (other) _____

4. Think of a confrontation you commonly have with your child(ren). Maybe it's over bedtime, eating vegetables, or not watching certain TV shows. Draw a star on the following graph to show how long you usually wait and how angry you allow yourself to get before taking action.

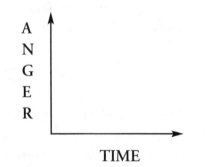

Now show on the following graph how you'd like the next confrontation to go.

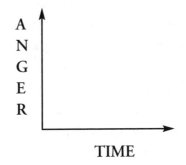

A
N
G
E
R

TIME

Try using the second graph as a goal this week. Use the space below to write a prayer about that goal.

TECH
SUPPORT
*get your questions
answered*

Q. Okay, I shouldn't use anger as a discipline tool. But won't my kids stop taking me seriously if I try to keep things light?

A. My answer may not be what you expected, but it represents something I've observed frequently and know to be valid. The *best* way to get children to do what you want is to spend time with them before disciplinary problems occur—having fun together and enjoying mutual laughter and joy. When those moments of love and closeness happen, kids are not as tempted to challenge and test the limits. Many confrontations can be avoided by building friendships with kids and thereby making them *want* to cooperate at home. It sure beats anger as a motivator of little ones!

—From *The New Dare to Discipline*

Q. How does this "anger vs. action" approach work with a teenager?

A. The general rule is to use action—not anger—to reach an understanding. Any time you can get teenagers to do what is necessary without becoming furious at them, you are ahead of the game. Let me provide a few examples of how this might be accomplished.

1. In Russia, I'm told that teenagers who are convicted of using drugs are denied driver's licenses for years. It is a very effective approach.

2. When my daughter was a teenager, she used to slip into my bathroom and steal my razor, my shaving cream, my toothpaste, or my comb. Of course, she never brought them back. Then after she had gone to school, I would discover the utensils missing. There I was with wet hair or "fuzzy" teeth, trying to locate the confiscated items in her bathroom. It was no big deal, but it was irritating at the time. Can you identify?

I asked Danae a dozen times not to do this but to no avail. Thus, the phantom struck without warning one cold morning. I hid everything she needed to "put on her face" and then left for the office. My wife told me she had never heard such wails and moans as were uttered that day. Our daughter plunged desperately through bathroom drawers looking for her toothbrush, comb, and hair dryer. The problem never resurfaced.

3. A family living in a house with a small hot-water tank was continually frustrated by their teenager's endless showers. Screaming at him did no good. Once he was locked behind the bathroom door, he stayed in the steamy stall until the last drop of warm water had been drained. Solution? In midstream, Dad stopped the flow of hot

water by turning a valve at the tank. Cold water suddenly poured from the nozzle. Junior popped out of the shower in seconds. Henceforth, he tried to finish bathing before the faucet turned frigid.

4. A single mother couldn't get her daughter out of bed in the morning until she announced a new policy: The hot water would be shut off promptly at 6:30 A.M. The girl could either get up on time or bathe in ice water. Another mother had trouble getting her eight-year-old out of bed each morning. She then began pouring bowls of frozen marbles under the covers with him each morning. They gravitated to wherever his body lay. The boy arose quite quickly.

5. Instead of standing in the parking lot and screaming at students who drive too fast, school officials now put huge bumps in the road that jar the teeth of those who ignore them. It does the job quite nicely.

6. You as the parent have the car that a teenager needs, the money that he covets, and the authority to grant or withhold privileges. If push comes to shove, these chips can be exchanged for commitments to live responsibly, share the workload at home, and stay off little brother's back. This bargaining process works for younger kids, too. I like the "one-to-one" trade-off for television-viewing time. It permits a child to watch one minute of television for every minute spent reading.

The possibilities are endless, and they depend not at all on anger, threats, and unpleasantries.

—From *The Complete Marriage and Family Home Reference Guide*

CHAPTER 4

FINDING BALANCE
IN DISCIPLINE

HOME BASE
getting started

My own mother had an unusually keen understanding of good disciplinary procedures, as I have indicated. She was very tolerant of my childishness, and I found her reasonable on most issues. . . . But there was one matter on which she was absolutely rigid: She did not tolerate sassiness. She knew that back talk and what she called "lip" were a child's most potent weapon of defiance and had to be discouraged.

I learned very early that if I was going to launch a flippant attack on her, I had better be standing at least 12 feet away. This distance was necessary to avoid an instantaneous response—usually aimed at my backside.

The day I learned the importance of staying out of reach shines like a neon light in my mind. I made the costly mistake of sassing her when I was about four feet away. I knew I had crossed the line and wondered what she would do about it. It didn't take long to find out. Mom wheeled around to grab something with which to express her displeasure, and her hand landed on a girdle. Those were the days when a girdle was lined with rivets and mysterious panels. She drew back and swung that abominable garment in my direction, and I can still hear it whistling through the air. The intended blow caught me across the chest, followed by a multitude of straps and buckles, wrapping themselves around my midsection. She gave me an entire thrashing with one blow! But from that day forward, I measured my words carefully when addressing my mother. I never spoke disrespectfully to her again, even when she was seventy-five years old.

I have shared that story many times through the years, to an interesting response. Most people found it funny and fully understood the innocuous meaning of that moment. A few others, who never met my mother and had no knowledge of her great love for me, quickly condemned her for the abusiveness of that event. . . .

I am the only person on Earth who can report accurately the impact of my mother's action. I'm the only one who lived it. And I'm here to tell you that the girdle-blow was an act of love! . . . We both knew I richly deserved it. And that's why the momentary pain of that event did not assault my self-worth. Believe it or not, it made me feel loved. . . .

Now let me say the obvious. I can easily see how the same setting could have represented profound rejection and hostility of the first order. If I had not known I was loved . . . if I had not deserved the punishment . . . if I

had been frequently and unjustly struck for minor offenses
. . . I would have suffered serious damage from the same
whirring girdle. The minor pain was not the critical variable. The *meaning* of the event is what mattered.
—Dr. James Dobson, *The New Dare to Discipline*

YOUR STORY
discovering where you stand

1. If you had to choose, would you rather be called a
"permissive" parent or an "authoritarian" parent? Why?

Do you think you tend to be more permissive or more
authoritarian? Why?

On the following scale, circle a number to show how
comfortable you are with your answer to the previous
question.

Totally Comfortable					Extremely Uncomfortable				
1	2	3	4	5	6	7	8	9	10

2. Finish this sentence: If love is like a balloon, control
is like . . .

____ a pin.

____ a lead weight.

____ a string.

____ helium.

____ (other) _____.

3. When it comes to discipline, how well do you balance love and control? Draw yourself on the seesaw below to show your answer.

Love   △   **Control**

Now put an X on the seesaw to show where you think your child(ren) would draw you. Is there a difference? If so, why?

SCREEN TIME
discussing the video

1. If Goldilocks were peeking in as you parent, would she say that you . . .
___ had better be tougher?
___ should replace your chairs?
___ ought to lighten up?
___ are just right?
___ need to wash your windows?

2. It is necessary when the situation warrants it to . . .

correct or punish a child. If done properly it does not inflict punishment to a youngster.

3. Both positives and negatives have . . .

there place.

Positive: affirmation, nourishes the childs spirit.
negative: discipline, punishment.

4. Moms and dads who try to be eternally positive . . .

ignoring their childs behaviour deprives
child of the benefits of
correction.

5. When it comes to love and control, our goal should be . . . *to balence love + control*
positive and negative reactions.

6. Seeing things from your child's perspective can . . .

helps you respond properly.
Is he happy she wants to share your joy.
Is your child reacting that way because her lonely
Is she afraid because she wants the security of your embrace.

WORDWORKS
input from
the Bible

1. " 'I have surely heard Ephraim's moaning: "You disciplined me like an unruly calf, and I have been disciplined. Restore me, and I will return, because you are the LORD my God. After I strayed, I repented; after I came to understand, I beat my breast. I was ashamed and humiliated because I bore the disgrace of my youth."

" 'Is not Ephraim my dear son, the child in whom I delight? Though I often speak against him, I still remember him. Therefore my heart yearns for him; I have great compassion for him,' " declares the LORD (Jeremiah 31:18-20).

These verses describe the way God disciplined Ephraim, a people of the nation of Judah. How would you describe the relationship between God and Ephraim? How did God seem to feel about His people?

By the time this dialogue between Ephraim and God took place, what had Ephraim realized about discipline?

Does God seem more interested here in controlling His people or loving them? How are the two concepts connected? What kind of balance does He strike?

How does God's approach to discipline here compare with your own?

2. "In your struggle against sin, you have not yet resisted to the point of shedding your blood. And you have forgotten that word of encouragement that addresses you as sons:

'My son, do not make light of the Lord's discipline, and do not lose heart when he rebukes you, because the Lord disciplines those he loves, and he punishes everyone he accepts as a son.'

Endure hardship as discipline; God is treating you as sons. For what son is not disciplined by his father? If you are not disciplined (and everyone undergoes discipline), then you are illegitimate children and not true sons. Moreover, we have all had human fathers who disciplined us and we respected them for it. How much more should we submit to the Father of our spirits and live! Our fathers disciplined us for a little while as they thought best; but God disciplines us for our good, that we may share in his holiness" (Hebrews 12:4-10).

Does God's approach to discipline here sound loving to you? Why or why not?

If your parents didn't discipline you, what might you conclude about their feelings toward you?

Someone has said that the opposite of love isn't hate— it's indifference. How does this passage reflect that idea?

Do you think your children see your discipline as an expression of your love? Why or why not?

YOUR WAY
applying the principles

1. Dr. Dobson has suggested "getting behind your child's eyes" in order to see discipline situations from his or her perspective. Think of one confrontation you had with your child last week. By the set of eyes below, draw or write how you think your child saw the situation.

How close is that perspective to the way you saw it? If you'd realized your child's perspective at the time, how might it have affected your response?

2. Dr. Dobson points out that we need both the positive and the negative to make parenting work, and that the two "charges" need to be balanced. Here's a car battery with positive and negative terminals. Draw two cables, one attached to each terminal. Draw each cable long or short to show whether you tend to emphasize the positive (praise, fun times, etc.), or the negative (penalties, warnings, etc.). Would you like to change this to make it more balanced? Why or why not?

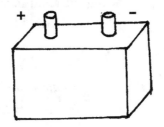

3. If you're parenting with your spouse, complete the following sentences and share them with him or her.

• When it comes to the strictness of our discipline, you and I tend to differ . . .

• I need help to understand why your approach to discipline is more . . .

• Maybe we can balance each other in this area by . . .

• Let's agree in advance on how we'll handle the following discipline situation this week:

4. When you discipline your children, do they understand that you disapprove of their behavior—but that you're not rejecting them personally? Think of a discipline situation you encountered during the last week. Try writing the child involved a poem or note assuring him or her of your love. Here's an example to get you started.

> *Roses are red, violets are blue;*
> *We didn't see eye to eye, me and you;*
> *You went to time-out when you fussed about chores;*
> *You said it was boring to vacuum the floors.*
> *I just want you to know when I discipline you,*
> *I love you still; that will always be true.*

Your poem or note:

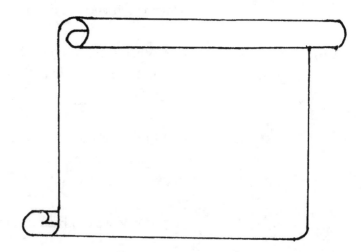

TECH SUPPORT
get your questions answered

Q. I'm not always sure my kids are actually defying me when they gripe about what I tell them to do. Should I crack down on them every time they resist doing what I tell them?

A. No. Defiance can be very different in origin from the "challenging" response I've been describing. A child's negativism may be caused by frustration, disappointment, fatigue, illness, or rejection and therefore must be interpreted as a warning signal to be heeded. Perhaps the toughest task in parenthood is to recognize the difference between these behavioral messages. A child's resistant behavior always contains a message to his parents, which they must decode before responding.

For example, the disobedient youngster may be saying, "I feel unloved now that I'm stuck with that screaming baby brother. Mom used to care for me; now nobody wants me. I hate everybody." When this kind of message underlies the defiance, the parents should move quickly to pacify its cause. The art of good parenthood, then, revolves around the interpretation of behavior.

—From *The Complete Marriage and Family Home Reference Guide*

Q. I think my husband is too tough on our kids; he thinks I'm too soft on them. Sometimes we disagree on our discipline and argue in front of them. What should we do?

A. You and your husband should present a united front, especially when children are watching. If you disagree on an issue, it can be discussed later in private. Unless the two of you can come to a consensus, your children will begin to perceive that standards of right and wrong are arbitrary. They will also make an "end run" around the tougher parent to get the answers they want. There are even more serious consequences for boys and girls when parents are radically different in their approach.

Here's the point of danger: Some of the most hostile, aggressive teenagers I've seen have come from family constellations where the parents have leaned in opposite directions in their discipline. Suppose the father is unloving and disinterested in the welfare of his kids. His approach is harsh and physical. He comes home tired and may knock them around if they get in his way. The mother is permissive by nature. She worries every day about the lack of love in the father-child relationship. Eventually she sets out to compensate for it. When Dad sends their son to bed without his dinner, Mom slips him milk and cookies. When he says no to a particular request, she finds a way to say yes. She lets the kids get away with murder because it is not in her spirit to confront them.

What happens under these circumstances is that the authority figures in the family contradict and cancel out each other. Consequently, the child is caught in the middle and often grows up hating both. It doesn't always work that way, but the probability for trouble is high. The middle ground between extremes of love and control must be sought if we are to produce healthy, responsible children.

—From *The Complete Marriage and Family Home Reference Guide*

CHAPTER 5

TO SPANK OR NOT TO SPANK

HOME BASE
getting started

[Spanking] has been the subject of heated controversy in recent years. More foolishness has been written on this subject than all other aspects of child rearing combined. Consider the views of Dr. John Valusek, a psychologist with whom I appeared on the Phil Donahue television show [as quoted in *Parade* magazine]:

> The way to stop violence in America is to stop spanking children, argues psychologist John Valusek. In a speech to the Utah Association for Mental Health some weeks ago, Valusek declared that parental spanking promotes the thesis that violence against others is acceptable.
> "Spanking is the first half-inch on the yardstick of

violence," said Valusek. "It is followed by hitting and ultimately by rape, murder, and assassination. The modeling behavior that occurs at home sets the stage: 'I will resort to violence when I don't know what else to do.' "

To Dr. Valusek and his permissive colleagues I can only say, "Poppycock!" How ridiculous to blame America's obsession with violence on the disciplinary effects of loving parents! This conclusion is especially foolish in view of the bloody fare offered to our children on television each day. The average sixteen-year-old has watched 18,000 murders during his formative years, including a daily bombardment of knifings, shootings, hangings, decapitations, and general dismemberment. Thus, it does seem strange that the psychological wizards of our day search elsewhere for the cause of brutality—and eventually point the finger of blame at the parents who are diligently training our future responsible citizens. Yet this is the kind of "press" that has been given in recent years to parents who believe in spanking their disobedient children.

—Dr. James Dobson in *The Strong-Willed Child*

YOUR STORY
discovering where you stand

1. When you hear the terms "corporal punishment" and "spanking," which of the following words spring to mind? Circle all that apply.

Deserved	Paddle	Authority
Violent	Hand	Belt
Stern	Pain	Mean
Cruel	Crying	Necessary
Justified	Correction	Good
Abuse	Smack	Bad

2. Take a guess: How many times do you think you were spanked when you were a child?

Take another guess: How many times do you think you've spanked your child(ren)?

Do you see any connection between your previous two answers? If so, what is it?

3. Let's say a neighbor saw you spanking your child. How would you feel? Why?

4. Try completing the following sentences.

a. Spanking would be unfair when . . .

b. My policy on spanking is . . .

c. I would spank my child(ren) if . . .

d. If you spank, you should use . . .

e. Spanking causes kids to . . .

f. The difference between spanking and child abuse is . . .

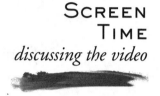

SCREEN
TIME
discussing the video

1. "Corporal Punishment" could be defined as . . .
___ beating a child when he deserves it
___ child abuse
___ an unfortunate but necessary evil
_✓_ a tool for correcting in love
___ (other) _____

2. We should spank when . . .

misbehaviour is willful.

3. We shouldn't spank if . . .

we are angry
or out of control
emotionally.

4. Corporal punishment works because . . .

it teaches the child
what is expected.

5. Minor pain teaches a child to . . .

avoid making the same
mistake again.

WORDWORKS
input from the Bible

1. "The rod of correction imparts wisdom, but a child left to himself disgraces his mother" (Proverbs 29:15).

Why do you suppose correction is described as a "rod" here?

Do parents ever spank children for reasons other than correction? What might some of those reasons be?

According to this verse, what happens when parents don't correct their children? How might this look in real life?

2. "He who spares the rod hates his son, but he who loves him is careful to discipline him" (Proverbs 13:24).

Dr. Dobson writes that spanking is an appropriate method of discipline for many children in response to willful defiance. Does this seem like a loving response to you? Why or why not?

Do you think most parents today would agree with this verse? Why or why not?

3. "Do not withhold discipline from a child; if you punish him with the rod, he will not die. Punish him with the rod and save his soul from death" (Proverbs 23:13, 14).

How might a parent misuse this passage to try to justify child abuse?

How could spanking be more merciful than *not* spanking? Can you give a real-life example?

4. "Discipline your son, and he will give you peace; he will bring delight to your soul" (Proverbs 29:17).

How could a careful use of spanking bring peace and delight to a parent's relationship with a child? Have you ever seen this happen?

YOUR WAY
applying the
principles

1. Dr. Dobson has written, "Appropriate spanking is the shortest and most effective route to an attitude adjustment."

How do you feel about that statement? Have you found it to be true? Are there times when it hasn't worked in your home?

2. If you and your spouse parent together, how do the two of you see spanking as a means of discipline? Fill in the following boxes to show how you both feel about spanking.

I Think Spanking Should Be Used . . .

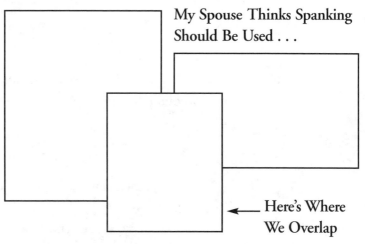

My Spouse Thinks Spanking Should Be Used . . .

← **Here's Where We Overlap**

3. Try formulating a "Corporal Punishment Code" to guide your use of spanking. Include types of behavior you think warrant the use of spanking, and limits you want to place on your use of such disciplinary measures. If you parent with a spouse, work together on this exercise. Here are some ideas to start you out:

Corporal Punishment Code

I / We, _____, in order to form a more perfect family and ensure domestic tranquility, do hereby set and establish this Code.

The following behaviors generally will be penalized by spanking:

Spankings will be delivered by the following means:

These are the limits we set for ourselves in regard to corporal punishment:

Established this _____ day of _____.

4. Do any of your children fall into the following categories? Mark your answers.
   ___ Child under 18 months
   ___ Teenager
   ___ Child with ADD, ADHD, or other neural problem
   ___ Child who was formerly abused
   ___ Very sensitive child

If you marked any of these choices, what alternatives to corporal punishment will you use as needed this week?

Tech Support
get your questions answered

Q. My daughter just celebrated her first birthday. She seems to have picked up the habit of throwing her toys across the room, even when I ask her not to. She'll even smile when she puts something from the floor into her mouth when I've said "No!" Should I spank her?

A. There is no excuse for spanking babies or children younger than fifteen to eighteen months of age. Even shaking an infant can cause brain damage and death at that delicate age! But midway through the second year (eighteen months), boys and girls become capable of knowing what you're telling them to do or not do. They can then very gently be held responsible for how they behave. Suppose a child is reaching for an electric socket or something that will hurt him. You say, "No!" but he just looks at you and continues reaching toward it. You can see the mischievous smile on his face as he thinks, *I'm going to do it anyway!* I'd encourage you to speak firmly so that he knows he is pushing past the limits. If he persists, slap his fingers just enough to sting. A small amount of pain goes a long way at that age and begins to introduce children to realities of the physical world and the importance of listening to what you say.

Through the next eighteen months, you gradually

establish yourself as the benevolent boss who means what you say and says what you mean. Contrary to what you have read in popular literature, this firm but loving approach to child rearing will *not* harm a toddler or make him violent. To the contrary, it is most likely to produce a healthy, confident child.

—From *The Complete Marriage and Family Home Reference Guide*

Q. I've spanked my children for their disobedience, and it didn't seem to help. Does this approach fail with some kids?

A. Children are so tremendously variable that it is sometimes hard to believe that they are all members of the same human family. Some kids can be crushed with nothing more than a stern look; others seem to require strong and even painful disciplinary measures to make a vivid impression. This difference usually results from the degree to which a child needs adult approval and acceptance. The primary parental task is to see things as the child perceives them, thereby tailoring the discipline to his or her unique needs. Accordingly, a boy or girl should never be so likely to be punished as when he or she knows it is deserved.

In a direct answer to your question, disciplinary measures usually fail because of fundamental errors in their application. It is possible for twice the amount of punishment to yield half the results. I have made a study of situations in which parents have told me that their children disregard the threat of punishment and continue to misbehave. There are four basic reasons for this lack of success:

1. The most common error is whimsical discipline. When the rules change every day and when punishment

for misbehavior is capricious and inconsistent, the effort to change behavior is undermined. There is no inevitable consequence to be anticipated. This entices children to see if they can beat the system. In society at large, it also encourages criminal behavior in those who believe they will not face the bar of justice.

2. Sometimes a child is more strong-willed than his parent—and they both know it. He just might be tough enough to realize that a confrontation with his mom or dad is really a struggle of wills. If he can withstand the pressure and not buckle during a major battle, he can eliminate that form of punishment as a tool in the parent's repertoire. Does he think through this process on a con-scious level? Usually not, but he understands it intuitively. He realizes that a spanking *must not* be allowed to succeed. Thus, he stiffens his little neck and guts it out. He may even refuse to cry and may say, "That didn't hurt." The parent concludes in exasperation, "Spanking doesn't work for my child."

3. The spanking may be too gentle. If it doesn't hurt, it doesn't motivate a child to avoid the consequence next time. A slap with the hand on the bottom of a multidia-pered thirty-month-old is not a deterrent to anything. Be sure the child gets the message—while being careful not to go too far.

4. For a few children, spankings are simply not effec-tive. The child who has attention deficit/hyperactivity dis-order (ADHD), for example, may be even more wild and unmanageable after corporal punishment. Also, the child who has been abused may identify loving discipline with the hatred of the past. Finally, the very sensitive child might need a different approach. Let me emphasize once

more that children are unique. The only way to raise them correctly is to understand each boy or girl as an individual and design parenting techniques to fit the needs and characteristics of that particular child.
　　—From *The Complete Marriage and Family Home Reference Guide*

CHAPTER 6

COMPLIANT VS. DEFIANT

HOME BASE
getting started

When there are two children in the family, it is likely that one youngster will be compliant and the other defiant. The easygoing child is often a genuine charmer. He smiles at least sixteen hours a day and spends most of his time trying to figure out what his parents want and how he can make them happy. In reality, he *needs* their praise and approval; thus his personality is greatly influenced by this desire to gain their affection and recognition.

The second child is approaching life from the opposite vantage point. He is sliding all four brakes and trying to gain control of the family steering mechanism. And don't you see how these differences in temperament lay the foundation for serious sibling rivalry and resentment? The defiant child faces constant discipline and hears many threats and finger-wagging lectures, while his angelic brother, little Goody-Two-Shoes, polishes his halo and soaks up the warmth of parental approval. . . .

I have found that the parents of compliant children don't understand their friends with defiant youngsters. They intensify guilt and anxiety [in parents of defiant children] by implying, "If you would raise your kids the way I do it, you wouldn't be having those awful problems." May I say to both groups that the willful child can be difficult to control even when his parents handle him with great skill and dedication.

—Dr. James Dobson in *The Strong-Willed Child*

YOUR STORY
discovering where you stand

1. When you were a kid, do you think you were "strong-willed" or "compliant"? Tell a quick story on yourself here to explain your answer.

Once upon a time . . .

2. As your parents encountered your defiance or compliance, what road signs do you think best describe how they responded? Circle your choices.

Stop   One Way
Yield   Watch for Falling Rocks

Obey Your Signal Only   Slow
Construction Zone   Rest Area
Emergency Vehicles Only   No Parking

Could any road signs represent ways in which they might have responded more positively? Make a check mark by those signs.

3. What about your child(ren)? Put each of your children's names under the appropriate headings below.

Compliant Child   **Strong-Willed Child**

Mark an "X" by the child who gets the most attention because of his or her compliance or defiance.

Now put an "L" by the names of your children who seem to be leaders and an "F" by those you think are followers.

4. If you have at least one strong-willed child, which of the following song titles best describes your feelings about that?

____ "Nobody Knows the Trouble I've Seen"
____ "I'm Sorry"
____ "We're Not Gonna Take It"
____ "Let's Give the Boy a Hand"

___ "Everything Is Beautiful"
___ "Mr. Big Stuff"
___ "Go Away, Little Girl"
___ "Land of Confusion"

SCREEN TIME
discussing the video

1. As described in the video, the temperament of defiant children is like . . .
___ a squeaky bike chain.
___ a broken-down car.
___ a viral disease.
___ a soggy cracker.
___ a careening shopping cart.

2. It's important to shape your child's will because . . .

3. To shape your child's will you should . . .

4. It's important to make a distinction between the strong-willed and compliant child in order to . . .
Raise them properly

5. The "blank slate" hypothesis is . . .

6. The best news to parents raising a strong-willed child is . . .

lead from young age

WORDWORKS
input from the Bible

1. "What do you think? There was a man who had two sons. He went to the first and said, 'Son, go and work today in the vineyard.'

" 'I will not,' he answered, but later he changed his mind and went. Then the father went to the other son and said the same thing. He answered, 'I will, sir,' but he did not go. Which of the two did what his father wanted?"

"The first," they answered (Matthew 21:28-31).

In the above story told by Jesus, do you think either of the sons was compliant? Defiant? Why?

Would you call either son a "strong-willed child"? Why or why not?

Suppose the father, before the events of the story, had labeled the first son as defiant and the second as compliant. Would the events have changed his mind? Why or why not?

How do you think the father should deal with the sons' responses to his direction?

2. "Adam lay with his wife Eve, and she became pregnant and gave birth to Cain. She said, 'With the help of the LORD I have brought forth a man.' Later she gave birth to his brother Abel.

"Now Abel kept flocks, and Cain worked the soil. In the course of time Cain brought some of the fruits of the soil as an offering to the LORD. But Abel brought fat portions from some of the firstborn of his flock. The LORD looked with favor on Abel and his offering, but on Cain and his offering he did not look with favor. So Cain was very angry, and his face was downcast.

"Then the LORD said to Cain, 'Why are you angry? Why is your face downcast? If you do what is right, will you not be accepted? But if you do not do what is right, sin is crouching at your door; it desires to have you, but you must master it'" (Genesis 4:1-7).

Cain brought "some" of his produce as an offering; Abel brought the *best* of his flock. How might their actions indicate compliance or defiance?

How did being strong-willed seem to affect Cain's response to God's correction?

In your experience, how does a strong-willed child tend to react to advice or criticism?

Why might the parent of a strong-willed child be reluctant to correct or discipline him or her?

What might be the result of failing to discipline a strong-willed child?

YOUR WAY
applying the
principles

1. After watching the video, do you need to change your characterization of your child(ren) from compliant to strong-willed or vice versa? If so, note the changes here:

Compliant Child   **Strong-Willed Child**

2. Is it sometimes hard to appreciate your child's personality? Try coming up with positive traits that start with the letters in "compliant" or "strong-willed" (depending on your child's personality). Share these with your child(ren) to let them know you appreciate their uniqueness. Examples are included to get you started.

Cooperative	S
O	T
M	Resolute
Patient	O
L	N
I	G
A	W
N	I
T	L
	L
	E
	Determined

3. It's good to balance the attention given to compliant and strong-willed kids, even when the latter tend to

demand more of it. If you were an advertiser with one product that was getting more attention than another, how would you assure the other product would receive its share? Try writing an "ad slogan" promoting the worthiness of each of your kids.

4. If you're a parent of one or more strong-willed children, which of the following thoughts would be most encouraging to you this week?

___ "It's not my fault!"

___ "I'm not the victim of some cruel cosmic joke!"

___ "I'm not the only one!"

___ "This, too, shall pass!"

___ (other) _____

How will you remind yourself of that thought this week?

TECH SUPPORT
get your questions answered

Q. Is it my imagination, or could my child be strong-willed even though she's only six months old?

A. Yes, Virginia, there *are* easy babies and there are difficult babies! Some seem determined to dismantle the homes into which they were born; they sleep cozily during the day and then howl in protest all night; they get colic and spit up the vilest stuff on their clothes (usually on the way to church); they control their internal plumbing until you hand them to strangers, and then let it blast. Instead of cuddling into the fold of the arms when being held, they stiffen rigidly in search of freedom. And to be honest, a mother may find herself leaning sockeyed over a vibrating crib at 3 A.M., asking the eternal question, "What's it all about, Alfie?" A few days earlier she was wondering, "Will he survive?" Now she is asking, "Will *I* survive?" But believe it or not, both generations will probably recover and this disruptive beginning will be nothing but a dim memory for the parents in such a brief moment. And from that demanding tyrant will grow a thinking, loving human being with an eternal soul and a special place in the heart of the Creator. To the exhausted and harassed new mother, let me say, "Hang tough! You are doing *the* most important job in the universe!"

—From *The Strong-Willed Child*

Q. Okay, I understand the strong-willed child better than I did. But tell me how to get our son through these years. He is tough as nails. What specific suggestions do you have for us?

A. Here is a summary of some approaches or ideas that I think are important:

1. You should not blame yourself for the temperament with which your child was born. He (or she) is simply a tough kid to handle, and your task is to rise to the challenge.

2. He is in greater danger because of his inclination to test the limits and scale the walls. Your utmost diligence and wisdom will be required to deal with him.

3. If you fail to understand his lust for power and independence, you can exhaust your resources and bog down in guilt. It will benefit no one.

4. For parents who have just begun, take charge of your babies. Hold tightly to the rein of authority in the early days, and build an attitude of respect during your brief window of opportunity. You will need every ounce of "awe" you can get during the years to come. Once you have established your right to lead, begin to let go systematically, year by year.

5. Don't panic, even during the storms of adolescence. Better times are ahead.

6. Don't let your son get too far from you emotionally. Stay in touch. Don't write him off, even when every impulse is to do just that. He needs you now more than ever before.

7. Give him time to find himself, even if he appears not to be searching.

8. Most important, I urge you to hold your children before the Lord in fervent prayer throughout their years at home. I am convinced that there is no other source of confidence and wisdom in parenting. There is not enough knowledge in the books, mine or anyone else's, to counteract the evil that surrounds our kids today. Teenagers are confronted by drugs, alcohol, sex, and foul language wherever they turn. And, of course, the peer pressure on them is enormous. We must bathe them in prayer every day of their lives. The God who made your children will hear your petitions. He has promised to do so. After all, He loves them more than you do.

And a concluding word: Remember that anyone can raise the easy kid. Guiding an SWC through the rebellious years takes a pro with a lot of love to give. I'll bet you're up to the task!

    —From *The Complete Marriage and Family Home Reference Guide*

CHAPTER 7

B) When Your Child Finally Drives You Crazy

CHANGING DISCIPLINE AS YOUR CHILD GROWS, PART 1

HOME BASE
getting started

A little child at birth is, of course, completely helpless. The little guy lying in his crib can do nothing for himself: He doesn't roll over or hold his bottle. He can't say please or thank you, and he doesn't apologize for getting you up six times in one night. He doesn't even have to appreciate your efforts. In other words, a child begins his life in a state of complete and total dependency, and you are in his servitude.

About twenty years later, however, some dramatic changes should have occurred in that individual. He should have developed the skills and self-discipline necessary for successful adult living. He is expected to spend his money wisely, hold a job, be loyal to one spouse (if he's married), support the needs of his family, obey the laws of the land, and be a good citizen. In other words, during the short course of childhood, an individual should progress systematically from dependency to independence—from irresponsibility to responsibility.

The question is, how does little John or Nancy or Paul get from Position A to Position B? How does that magical transformation from babyhood to maturity take place? Some parents seem to believe that it all will coalesce toward the latter end of adolescence, about fifteen minutes before the individual leaves home. I reject that notion categorically. The best preparation for adulthood comes from training in responsibility during the childhood years.

—Dr. James Dobson in *The Complete Marriage and Family Home Reference Guide*

YOUR STORY
discovering where you stand

1. How did you picture parenting before you had your first child? Has it turned out to be different? Draw a family scene or symbols that represent the two versions:

Before:

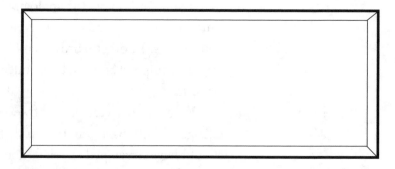

After:

If there are differences between the two drawings, are they due in part to the strength of your children's wills?

2. Which of the following shapes best represents the will you had as a young child? Circle your answer.

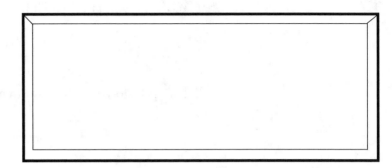

Which of those shapes best represents the will you were left with by the end of childhood? Put a check mark over your answer.

3. Did your parents "shape" your will? If so, how?

4. If shaping your child's will is like sculpting clay, what "tools" do you guess you'll need?

What tools do you think you may be missing?

5. Choose a phrase to complete the following sentence: When it comes to disciplining my child, my greatest fear is . . .

___ that I'll hurt him.

___ that I'll make her afraid of me or damage our relationship.

___ that I won't be able to discipline effectively.

___ (other) _____.

SCREEN TIME
discussing the video

1. According to the video, the babyhood and toddler years are. . . .

____ curious years/ exploration of their environment.

____ fragile years/approach discipline with sensitivity.

____ years to drive you crazy.

____ a time to give security, affection, and warmth.

____ not a time to "reason" with your child.

____ (other)_____.

2. When a child is an infant, discipline should look like . . .

3. When a child is a toddler, discipline should look like . . .

4. Mild corporal punishment should be used with a strong-willed toddler when . . .

5. A toddler should not be punished for touching something if . . .

6. These beginning years are an important time to instill . . .

WORDWORKS
input from
the Bible

1. "[A church overseer] must manage his own family well and see that his children obey him with proper respect" (1 Timothy 3:4).

What do you think a well-managed family looks like?

How can you tell when your children are obeying you with "proper respect?"

Do these two goals seem achievable to you? Why or why not?

2. "He who ignores discipline despises himself, but whoever heeds correction gains understanding" (Proverbs 15:32).

"Whoever loves discipline loves knowledge, but he who hates correction is stupid" (Proverbs 12:1).

What do these verses teach us about the importance of discipline?

About the possible consequences of a lack of discipline?

3. "Train a child in the way he should go, and when he is old he will not turn from it" (Proverbs 22:6).

What's the value of appropriate discipline early in life?

Do you wish someone had done more to teach you discipline when you were growing up? Why or why not?

YOUR WAY
applying the principles

1. Here are some instances in which your child might defy your authority. How will you meet the challenge? Make a check mark next to the confrontations you think are worth pursuing. After each of those, tell how you might deal with the circumstance.

____ Your two-year-old looks you in the eye as he dumps the potted plant on the floor.
  Battle plan:

____ Your four-year-old refuses to wear the green outfit and wants to wear the blue one.
  Battle plan:

____ Your toddler wants to wear a bathing suit today even though it's 38 degrees outside.
  Battle plan:

____ Your three-year-old keeps trying to stick the screwdriver into the electrical outlet.
  Battle plan:

_____ You are at a restaurant and you want your child to eat a veggie with dinner; he wants dessert instead.
Battle plan:

TECH SUPPORT
get your questions answered

Q. My child just entered the "terrible twos." I understand now what everyone was warning me about. What advice do you have for discipline during these "wonder years"?

A. Perhaps the most frustrating aspect of the "terrible twos" is the tendency of kids to spill things, destroy things, eat horrible things, fall off things, flush things, kill things, and get into things. They also have a knack for doing embarrassing things, like sneezing on a nearby man at a lunch counter. During these toddler years, any unexplained silence of more than thirty seconds can throw an adult into a sudden state of panic. What mother has not had the thrill of opening the bedroom door, only to find Tony Tornado covered with lipstick from the top of his pink head to the carpet on which he stands? On the wall is his own artistic creation with a red handprint in the center, and throughout the room is the aroma of Chanel No. 5 with which he has anointed his baby brother. . . .

You *must* keep a sense of humor during the twos and threes in order to preserve your own sanity. But you must also proceed with the task of instilling obedience and respect for authority. . . . Although the "older" toddler is much different physically and emotionally than he was at eighteen months, the tendency to test and challenge parental authority is still very much in evidence. In fact, when the young toddler consistently wins the early confrontations and conflicts, he becomes even more difficult to handle in the second and third years. Then a lifelong disrespect for authority often begins to settle into his young mind. Therefore, I cannot overemphasize the importance of instilling two distinct messages within your child before he is forty-eight months of age: (1) "I love you more than you can possibly understand. You are precious to me, and I thank God every day that He let me raise you!" (2) "Because I love you, I must teach you to obey me. That is the only way I can take care of you and protect you from things that might hurt you. Let's read what the Bible tells us: 'Children, obey your parents, for this is right.'" (Ephesians 6:1) . . .

Specifically, how does one discipline a "naughty" two- or three-year-old child? One possible approach is to require the boy or girl to sit in a chair and think about what he has done. Most children of this age are bursting with energy and absolutely hate to spend ten dull minutes with their wiggly posteriors glued to a chair. To some individuals, this form of punishment can be even more effective than a spanking, and is remembered longer.

—From *The Strong-Willed Child*

Q. How can I really tell when my child is being defiant?

A. "But how can you know for sure?" That question has been asked of me hundreds of times. A mother will say, "I think Chuckie was being disrespectful when I told him it was bath-time, but I'm not sure what he was thinking."

There is a very straightforward solution to this parental dilemma: use the first occasion for the purpose of clarifying the next. Say to your son, "Chuck, your answer to me just now sounded sassy. I'm not sure how you intended it. But so we will understand each other, don't talk to me like that again." If it occurs again, you'll know it was deliberate.

—From *The New Strong-Willed Child*

CHAPTER 8

A) To Be Sure Your Child Is Seen
And Not Heard

CHANGING DISCIPLINE
AS YOUR CHILD
GROWS, PART 2

HOME BASE
getting started

The most urgent advice I can give to the parents of an
assertive, independent child is to establish their positions
as strong but loving leaders when Junior and Missy are in
the preschool years. This is the first step toward helping
them learn to control their powerful impulses. Alas, there
is no time to lose. A naturally defiant youngster is in a
high-risk category for antisocial behavior later in life. She
is more likely to challenge her teachers in school and question the values she has been taught. Her temperament
leads her to oppose anyone who tries to tell her what to
do. Fortunately, this outcome is not inevitable, because the
complexities of the human personality make it impossible

to predict behavior with complete accuracy. But the probabilities lie in that direction.

—Dr. James Dobson in *The New Strong-Willed Child*

YOUR STORY
discovering where you stand

1. Take a look at the following list of words and phrases. Think back to when you were a preschooler. Which words and phrases reflect the way you were disciplined then, and your feelings about discipline at the time? Underline those words and phrases. Next, recall your elementary school days. Circle the words and phrases that relate to your discipline during that stage. Finally, remember when you were a teenager. Draw a box around words and phrases that describe the way you were disciplined then, and how you felt about it. (Feel free to select the same words and phrases more than once if necessary.)

"It's not fair!"   Time-outs   "You're grounded!"
"I can't wait to move out!"   "No allowance this week!"
Sitting in the corner   spanking   "Don't touch!"
"You don't understand me!"   "Ouch!"   Pouting
"Wait till your father gets home!"   Handslap
"But I didn't do it!"   "That didn't hurt!"
"As long as you live under my roof, you'll obey my rules!"
"That's a no-no!"   Gold stars   "Go to your room!"
"I hate you!"   Losing privileges   Lectures
"No car keys till you get your grades up!"   "No dessert!"
"That will cost you a dollar!"   "No TV for three days!"
"Get off my case!"   Nagging   Natural consequences
"What a good boy (or girl)!"   "Because I said so!"
"Here's a piece of candy for obeying!"   Extra chores
"They'll never find out!"   "Quit treating me like a baby!"

What do your answers tell you about discipline?

About kids?

About growing up?

2. How old were your children when you started disciplining them?

How old do you think they'll be when you stop?

3. Are there disciplinary tactics that used to work with your child but don't anymore? If so, what are they? Have you stopped using them?

Are there disciplinary tactics you didn't use until recently? Why did you start using them?

SCREEN TIME
discussing the video

1. The problem with ignoring negative attitudes is . . .

2. Respectful, responsible children are created by . . .

3. When a child moves into elementary age, discipline looks more like . . .

4. Our most important responsibility as parents might be . . .

5. By the time a child reaches 9, discipline has changed to include . . .

6. The way to connect behavior with consequences is to . . .

WORDWORKS
input from the Bible

1. "There is a time for everything, and a season for every activity under heaven:
  a time to be born and a time to die,
  a time to plant and a time to uproot,
  a time to kill and a time to heal,
  a time to tear down and a time to build,
  a time to weep and a time to laugh,
  a time to mourn and a time to dance,
  a time to scatter stones and a time to gather them,

> a time to embrace and a time to refrain,
> a time to search and a time to give up,
> a time to keep and a time to throw away,
> a time to tear and a time to mend,
> a time to be silent and a time to speak,
> a time to love and a time to hate,
> a time for war and a time for peace"

(Ecclesiastes 3:1-8).

According to these verses, different times call for different responses. When it comes to disciplining your child(ren), how could it be right at one time to "tear down" and right at another to "build"?

How could it be right at one time to "be silent" and right at another to "speak"?

How could it be right at one time to "embrace" and right at another to "refrain"?

How is disciplining a three-year-old different from disciplining a sixteen-year-old? Try working as many phrases from the Ecclesiastes verses into your answer as you can.

2. "When I was a child, I talked like a child, I thought like a child, I reasoned like a child. When I became a man, I put childish ways behind me" (1 Corinthians 13:11).

What could happen to a child whose parents discipline him without taking his changing mind and body into account?

Did your parents, in their approach to disciplining you, seem to realize the truth of this verse? Why or why not?

3. "Be completely humble and gentle; be patient, bearing with one another in love" (Ephesians 4:2).

Do you think it takes more patience to discipline a two-year-old or a teenager? Why?

Which of the aforementioned qualities—humility, gentleness, patience, or love—do you need most to help you cope with the changes occurring in your child(ren)?

YOUR WAY

applying the principles

1. Think of yourself as Dr. Mom or Dr. Dad. Your child has come to you with a "discipline deficiency." You can prescribe a variety of "medicines" (rewards, time-outs, spanking, loss of privileges, etc.). Remember as you prescribe, though, that the medicines and "dosages" will change depending on your child's age. What prescriptions will you write?

If you have an infant, your recommendation would be:

Medicines   **Dosages**

If you have a toddler, your recommendation would be:

Medicines   **Dosages**

If your child is elementary age, your recommendation would be:

Medicines   **Dosages**

If your child is an adolescent, your recommendation would be:

Medicines   **Dosages**

2. A goal of discipline, especially during the elementary years, is to shape your child's attitudes. Fill the heart below with attitudes you feel are important to instill in your child. Around the heart, jot down any ideas you have about how you'll accomplish that goal. If you parent with a spouse, work together on this.

3. Here are two "apron strings," representing your authority over your child(ren). On the first string, make marks to show the ages of your children. On the second string, make marks to show how deeply you've "cut the apron strings" for each child so far. Are you satisfied with

the rate at which you're replacing discipline with self-discipline in each child? Why or why not?

Age 0   *Age 21*

TECH SUPPORT
get your questions answered

Q: How can I acquaint my twelve-year-old with the need for responsible behavior throughout his life? He is desperately in need of this understanding.

A: One important objective during the preadolescent period is to teach the child that actions have inevitable consequences. One of the most serious casualties in a permissive society is the failure to connect those two factors, behavior and consequences. A three-year-old child screams insults at his mother, but Mom stands blinking her eyes in confusion. A first grader defies his teacher, but the school makes allowances for his age and takes no action. A ten-year-old is caught stealing candy in a store but is released to the recognizance of her parents. A fifteen-year-old sneaks the keys to the family car, but her father pays the fine when she is arrested. A seventeen-year-old drives his Chevy like a maniac, and his parents pay for the repairs when he wraps it around a telephone pole. All through childhood, loving parents seem determined to intervene between behavior and consequences, breaking the connection and preventing the valuable learning that could and should have occurred.

How does one connect behavior with consequences?

By being willing to let the child experience a reasonable amount of pain or inconvenience when he behaves irresponsibly. The best approach is to expect boys and girls to carry the responsibility that is appropriate for their age and occasionally to taste the bitter fruit that irresponsibility bears. In so doing, behavior is wedded to consequences, just like in real life.

—From *The Complete Marriage and Family Home Reference Guide*

CHAPTER 9

PROTECTING THE SPIRIT

HOME BASE
getting started

Our objective, then, is not simply to shape the will, *but to do so without breaking the spirit. . . .*

The will is malleable. It can and should be molded and polished—not to make a robot of a child for our selfish purposes, but to give him the ability to control his *own* impulses and exercise self-discipline later in life. In fact, we have a God-given responsibility as parents to shape the will. . . .

On the other hand (and let me give this paragraph the strongest possible emphasis), the *spirit* of a child is a million times more vulnerable than his will. It is a delicate flower that can be crushed and broken all too easily (and even unintentionally). The spirit, as I have defined it, relates to the self-esteem or the personal worth that a child feels. It is *the* most fragile characteristic in human nature, being particularly vulnerable to rejection and ridicule and failure.

How, then, are we to shape the will while preserving the spirit intact? It is accomplished by establishing reasonable boundaries and enforcing them with love, but by avoiding any implication that the child is unwanted, unnecessary, foolish, ugly, dumb, a burden, an embarrassment, or a disastrous mistake. Any accusation that assaults the worth of a child in this way can be costly, such as "You are so stupid!" Or, "Why can't you make decent grades in school like your sister?" Or, "You have been a pain in the neck ever since the day you were born!" . . .

One more time: The goal in dealing with a difficult child is to shape the will without breaking the spirit.

—Dr. James Dobson in *The New Strong-Willed Child*

YOUR STORY
discovering where you stand

1. When you were growing up, what messages did your parents seem to be sending when they were disciplining you? Check all that apply.

___ "This hurts me more than it hurts you."

___ "You're a bad kid."

___ "I'm doing this because I care about you."

___ "I hate you."

___ "What you did was wrong, but I love you."

___ "You drive me crazy."

___ "Dr. Dobson made me do this."

Did your parents do anything to let you know they loved you after you'd been disciplined? How do you feel about that now?

2. How would you complete this sentence? When I discipline, I try to show my kids I love them by . . .

____ giving them money or hot chocolate.

____ giving them a hug.

____ saying, "I love you."

____ promising never to discipline them again.

____ (other) _____.

3. How much do you yell at your kids during a typical week? Mark your answer on the scale below.

The Yell-O-Meter

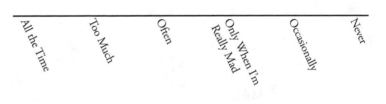

What message do you think this sends to your child(ren)?

4. How much do you listen to your kids during a typical week? Mark your answer on the scale below.

The Hear-O-Meter

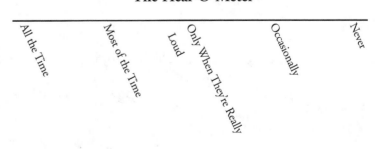

What message do you think this sends to your child(ren)?

5. When do you find it hardest to listen to your kids? What do you do at those times?

SCREEN TIME

discussing the video

1. When it comes to shaping your child's will, are you a . . .

___ sculptor?
___ demolition expert?
___ bull in a china shop?
___ brain surgeon?
___ (other) _____?

2. According to Dr. Dobson, the goal of dealing with a difficult child is to . . . *Shape the will w/o breaking the spirit*

3. The way to shape the will without attacking a child's spirit is . . .

- establish boundaries in advance

- Don't insult the worth of your child
- handle spirit with great care

4. When a child seems out of control, he or she is asking . . . *for help*
- begging for intervention to shape his will
- need to set boundaries & enforce rules

5. The pairing of love and consistent discipline is . . .

- its essential in not breaking their spirit

- ensure child

- Always be consistent
- Don't lack the courage to do battle

WORDWORKS
input from
the Bible

1. "Fathers, do not exasperate your children; instead, bring them up in the training and instruction of the Lord" (Ephesians 6:4).

This teaching from the Bible can fit moms and dads alike. So think about this: In what ways might you exasperate your children?

- expect too much from them, enough doesn't satisfy the parents
- Parents don't practice what they preach
- failure to listen to their side - Hear out your children

This verse implies that it's possible to train and instruct kids without exasperating them. Try naming ten ways to do that. We've provided three to get you started.

• Making Bible study fun
• Explaining reasons for discipline
• Getting kids' feedback
•
•

- •
- •
- •
- •
- •

2. "It is not good to punish an innocent man, or to flog officials for their integrity" (Proverbs 17:26).

Were you ever unjustly corrected or punished? What were your feelings at that moment?

Do you think your children ever feel unjustly corrected or punished? How do you help them deal with those feelings?

3. "He will turn the hearts of the fathers to their children, and the hearts of the children to their fathers . . ." (Malachi 4:6)

Do you see this happening in your family?

In your country?

In the world?

How could protecting the spirits of our children help to reach this goal?

YOUR WAY
applying the
principles

1. Think of the last time you had to discipline your child(ren). Do you think you did better at shaping the will or breaking the spirit? Circle your answer on this scale.

The Sculpt-O-Meter

1	2	3	4	5	6	7	8	9	10

Shaped the will   Broke the spirit

If you leaned toward breaking the spirit, what could you have done differently?

2. Do you ever yell at your child(ren)? Which of the following tactics might help you most this week in treating your child(ren) with more respect?

___ Counting to ten before you speak

___ Sending your child to his or her room until you cool down

___ Asking your spouse to give you a signal when you're yelling

___ Fining yourself a dollar every time you yell

___ (other) _____

3. Answer this for each child you have (use a separate sheet if you have more than three). Label each thought balloon with the name of one of your children. Fill in the thought bubble with the answer to this question: When you discipline your child, what is he or she usually thinking and feeling?

If you knew the answer to this question, explain how you knew.

If you could answer with more certainty for some of your children than for others, why do you think that was?

If you drew a blank for all your kids, tell what you need to do about it.

TECH
SUPPORT
*get your questions
answered*

Q. I get very upset because my two-year-old boy will not sit still and be quiet in church. He knows he's not supposed to be noisy, but he hits his toys on the pew and sometimes talks out loud. Should I spank him for being disruptive?

A. Most two-year-olds can no more fold their hands

and sit quietly in church than they can swim the Atlantic Ocean. They squirm and churn and burn every second of their waking hours. No, this child should not be punished. He should be left in the nursery where he can shake the foundations without disturbing the worshipers.

—From *The New Strong-Willed Child*

Q. My four-year-old son came into the house and told me he had seen a lion in the backyard. He was not trying to be funny. He really tried to convince me that this lie was true and became quite upset when I didn't believe him. I want him to be an honest and truthful person. Should I have spanked him?

A. Definitely not. There is a very thin line between fantasy and reality in the mind of a preschool child, and they often confuse the two. I remember, for example, when I took my son to Disneyland when he was three years of age. He was absolutely terrified by the wolf who stalked around with the three pigs. Ryan took one look at those sharp, jagged teeth and screamed in terror. I have a priceless video of him scrambling for the safety of his mother's arms. After we returned home, I told Ryan there was a "very nice man" inside the wolf suit, who wouldn't hurt anyone. My son was so relieved by that news that he needed to hear it repeatedly.

He would say, "Dad?"

"What, Ryan?"

"Tell me 'bout that nice man!"

You see, Ryan was not able to distinguish between the fantasy character and a genuine threat to his health and safety. I would guess that the lion story related in the question above was a product of the same kind of confusion.

The child may well have believed that a lion was in the backyard. This mother would have been wise to play along with the game while making it perfectly clear that she didn't believe the story. She could have said, "Oh my goodness! A lion in the backyard! I sure hope he is a friendly old cat. Now, Jonathan, please wash your hands and come eat lunch."
—From *The New Strong-Willed Child*

Q. My ten-year-old often puts his milk glass too close to his elbow when eating, and has knocked it over at least six times. I keep telling him to move the glass, but he won't listen. When he spilt the milk again yesterday, I jerked him up and gave him a spanking with a belt. Today I don't feel good about the incident. Should I have reacted more patiently?

A. It is all too easy to tell a mother she shouldn't have become upset over something that happened yesterday. After all, I'm not the one who had to clean up the mess. However, your son did not intend to spill his milk and he was, in effect, punished for his irresponsibility. It would have been better to create a method of grabbing his attention and helping him remember to return his glass to a safe area. For example, you could have cut an "off limits" zone from red construction paper and taped it to the side of his plate. If Junior placed his glass on that paper, he would have to help wash the dishes after the evening meal. I guarantee you that he would seldom "forget" again. In fact, this procedure would probably sensitize him to the location of the glass, even after the paper was removed.
—From *The Strong-Willed Child*

CHAPTER 10

THE STRONG-WILLED ADOLESCENT, PART I

HOME BASE
getting started

I can understand why [many parents] look toward the adolescent years with some apprehension. This is a tough time to raise kids. Many youngsters sail right through that period with no unusual stresses and problems, but others get caught in a pattern of rebellion that disrupts families and scares their moms and dads to death. I've spent several decades trying to understand that phenomenon and how to prevent it. The encouraging thing is that the most rebellious teens usually grow up to be responsible and stable adults who can't remember why they were so angry in earlier days.

I once devoted a radio program to a panel of formerly rebellious teens that included three successful ministers, Rev. Raul Ries, Pastor Mike MacIntosh, and Rev. Franklin

Graham, son of Dr. Billy and Ruth Graham. Each of them had been a difficult adolescent who gave his parents fits. With the exception of Raul, who had been abused at home, the other two couldn't recall what motivated their misbehavior or why they didn't just go along and get along. That is often the way with adolescence. It's like a tornado that drops unexpectedly out of a dark sky, tyrannizes a family, shakes up the community, and then blows on by. Then the sun comes out and spreads its warmth again.

Even though the teen years can be challenging, they're also filled with excitement and growth. Rather than fearing that experience, therefore, I think you ought to anticipate it as a dynamic time when your kids transition from childhood to full-fledged adulthood.

—Dr. James Dobson in *The Complete Marriage and Family Home Reference Guide*

YOUR STORY
discovering where you stand

1. Let's take a trip down memory lane—to your own teenage years. See how many of the following you can recall:

Your favorite song:

Your favorite TV show:

How much a gallon of gasoline cost:

What your room smelled like:

A nickname your parents gave you:

When your parent(s) expected you to be home at night:

The penalty for getting home later than that:

The number of times you argued with your parent(s) in an average month:

How your parent(s) responded when you argued:

2. If you have a teenager now, try to complete the following as he or she would. (If you have more than one teen, give separate answers and label them with each young person's initials.)

When your parent(s) expect you to be home at night:

The penalty for getting home later than that:

The number of times you argue with your parent(s) in an average month:

How your parent(s) respond when you argue:

3. If you don't have teens yet, try answering these questions:

When will you expect your teen(s) to be home at night?

What will be the penalty for getting home later than that?

How many times do you think your teen will argue with you in an average month?

How will you respond when your teen argues with you?

4. Whether or not you have a teen, tell why you agree or disagree with this statement:

"ALL TEENAGERS ARE STRONG-WILLED."

SCREEN TIME

discussing the video

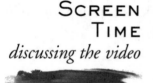

1. Your reaction to Sir Reginald Puffin-Smythe's search for a compliant adolescent:

___ It could happen.
___ Give up!
___ Come to my house to look.
___ Don't come to my house to look.
___ (other) _____.

Girls buff
Boys Puff

2. Children entering adolescence have volatile emotions because . . .

— mischevious hormones begin to enrage

3. It's important to help teens understand their physical changes because . . . *puberty*
their emotional changes begin to happen with their physical

4. Even greater than death, a teen's greatest fear is . . .
Rejection, humilition, terror of peer groups

5. The middle school years are probably the most critical to . . . *child development of mental health*

Always stand firm on moral issues

6. In parenting adolescents, our goal should be . . .
get them through adolescent stage and stay on your team

WORDWORKS
input from the Bible

1. "Every year his [Jesus'] parents went to Jerusalem for the Feast of the Passover. When he was twelve years old, they went up to the Feast, according to the custom. After the Feast was over, while his parents were returning home, the boy Jesus stayed behind in Jerusalem, but they were unaware of it. Thinking he was in their company, they traveled on for a day. Then they began looking for him among their relatives and friends. When they did not find him, they went back to Jerusalem to look for him. After three days they found him in the temple courts, sitting among the teachers, listening to them and asking them questions. Everyone who heard him was

amazed at his understanding and his answers. When his parents saw him, they were astonished. His mother said to him, 'Son, why have you treated us like this? Your father and I have been anxiously searching for you.'

"'Why were you searching for me?' he asked. 'Didn't you know I had to be in my Father's house?' But they did not understand what he was saying to them. Then he went down to Nazareth with them and was obedient to them" (Luke 2:41-51).

Would you say Jesus was being strong-willed here? How does His behavior compare to that of adolescents you've known?

Is it possible for a young person to be strong-willed and not defiant? How do you know?

Is it any comfort to you that even Jesus and His earthly parents didn't see eye-to-eye all the time? Why or why not?

2. "David said to Saul, 'Let no one lose heart on account of this Philistine [Goliath]; your servant will go and fight him.'

"Saul replied, 'You are not able to go out against this Philistine and fight him; you are only a boy, and he has been a fighting man from his youth.'

"But David said to Saul, 'Your servant has been keeping his father's sheep. When a lion or a bear came and carried off a sheep from the flock, I went after it, struck it and rescued the sheep from its mouth. When it turned on me, I seized it by its hair, struck it and killed it. Your servant has killed both the lion and the bear; this uncircumcised Philistine will be like one of them, because he has defied the armies of the living God. The LORD who delivered me from the paw of the lion and the paw of the bear will deliver me from the hand of this Philistine.'

"Saul said to David, 'Go, and the LORD be with you.'

"Then Saul dressed David in his own tunic. He put a coat of armor on him and a bronze helmet on his head. David fastened on his sword over the tunic and tried walking around, because he was not used to them.

"'I cannot go in these,' he said to Saul, 'because I am not used to them.' So he took them off. Then he took his staff in his hand, chose five smooth stones from the stream, put them in the pouch of his shepherd's bag and, with his sling in his hand, approached the Philistine. . . .

"So David triumphed over the Philistine with a sling and a stone; without a sword in his hand he struck down the Philistine and killed him." (1 Samuel 17:32-40, 50)

Would you say that young David was strong-willed? Why or why not?

What positive attributes of a strong-willed adolescent are displayed in this story?

David went on to be king of Israel. If you have (or someday have) a strong-willed teenager, what will be your hope for him or her?

YOUR WAY
applying the principles

1. Name one battle you think is worth fighting with your (present or future) teenager. Explain your answer.

Name one that you think doesn't quite make the rank of "great moral significance."

When you hear that you don't have to fight every battle that comes along, what's your reaction?

___ "That's a relief!"

___ "But you don't know my kid!"

___ "If I don't fight, who will?"

___ "I gave up a long time ago anyway."

___ (other) _____

What accounts for your answer?

2. If your teen had been one of the ones interviewed for this segment, and he or she was asked about how much communication you've had in the last week, which of the following do you think he or she would have answered?

___ I dunno.

___ Too much.

___ It's never enough.

___ What's it to you?

___ (other) _____

What do you think his or her most truthful answer would be?

3. What can you do to show that you're on your child's team? Pick one of the following options (or create your own) and try it this week.

___ Listen to his or her favorite music together.

___ Give him or her a coupon for one free room cleaning.

___ Make him or her a valentine card no matter what time of year it is.

___ Proudly introduce him or her to people at your workplace.

___ (other) _____

TECH SUPPORT

get your questions answered

Q. What would you do to encourage the cooperation of my thirteen-year-old, who deliberately makes a nuisance of himself? He throws his clothes around, refuses to help out with any routine tasks in the house, and pesters his little brother incessantly. How can I get his attention?

A. If any approach will succeed in charging his sluggish batteries or motivating him to live within the rules, it will probably involve an incentive-and-disincentive program of some variety. The following three steps might be helpful in initiating such a system:

1. Decide what is important to the youngster for use as a motivator. Two hours with the family car on date night is worth the world to a sixteen-year-old who has just gotten his or her license. (This could be the most expensive incentive in history if the young driver is a bit shaky behind the wheel.) An allowance is another easily available source of inspiration. Teenagers have a great need for cold cash today. A routine date . . . might cost $20 or more—in some cases far more. Yet another incentive may involve a fashionable article of clothing that would not ordinarily be within your teen's budget. Offering him or her a means of obtaining such luxuries is a happy alternative to the whining, crying, begging, complaining, and pestering that might occur

otherwise. Mom says, "Sure you can have the ski sweater, but you'll have to earn it." Once an acceptable motivator is agreed upon, the second step can be implemented.

2. Formalize the agreement. A contract is an excellent means of settling on a common goal. Once an agreement has been written, it is signed by the parent and teen. The contract may include a point system that enables your teenager to meet the goal in a reasonable time period. If you can't agree on the point values, you could allow for binding arbitration from an outside party. Let's examine a sample agreement in which Marshall wants a compact-disc player, but his birthday is ten months away, and he's flat broke. The cost of the player is approximately $150. His father agrees to buy the device if Marshall earns ten thousand points over the next six to ten weeks doing various tasks. Many of these opportunities are outlined in advance, but the list can be lengthened as other possibilities become apparent:

   a. For making bed and straightening room each morn-
      ing: 50 points
   b. For each hour of studying: 150 points
   c. For each hour of housecleaning or yard work done:
      300 points
   d. For being on time to breakfast and dinner: 40 points
   e. For baby-sitting siblings (without conflict) per hour:
      150 points
   f. For washing the car each week: 250 points
   g. For arising by 8:00 A.M. Saturday morning: 100
      points

While the principles are almost universally effective, the method of application must be varied. With a little imagination, you can create a list of chores and point values that work in your family. It's important to note that points can be gained for cooperation and lost for resist-ance. Disagreeable and unreasonable behavior can be penalized fifty points or more. (However, penalties must be imposed fairly and rarely or the entire system will crumble.) Also, bonus points can be awarded for behavior that is particularly commendable.

3. Finally, establish a method to provide immediate rewards. Remember that prompt reinforcement achieves the best results. This is necessary to sustain teens' interest as they move toward the ultimate goal. A thermometer-type chart can be constructed, with the point scale listed down the side. At the top is the ten-thousand-points mark, beside a picture of a compact-disc player or other prize. Each evening, the daily points are totaled and the red portion of the thermometer is extended upward. Steady, short-term progress might earn Marshall a bonus of some sort—per-haps a CD of his favorite musician or a special privilege. If he changes his mind about what he wishes to buy, the points can be diverted to another purchase. For example, five thousand points is 50 percent of ten thousand and would be worth $75 toward another purchase. However, do not give your child the reward if he does not earn it. That would eliminate future uses of reinforcement. Like-wise, do not deny or postpone the goal once it is earned.

This system described above is not set in concrete. It should be adapted to the age and maturity of the adoles-cent. One youngster would be insulted by an approach that would thrill another. Use your imagination and work out the details with your youngster. This suggestion won't work with every teenager, but some will find it exciting. Lots of luck to you.

—From *The Complete Marriage and Family Home Reference Guide*

CHAPTER 11

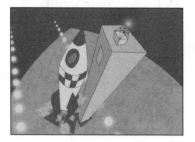

THE STRONG-WILLED ADOLESCENT, PART 2

HOME BASE
getting started

The philosophy we applied with our teenagers (and you might try with yours) can be called "loosen and tighten." By this I mean we tried to loosen our grip on everything that had no lasting significance and tighten down on everything that did. We said yes whenever we possibly could to give support to the occasional no. And most important, we tried never to get too far away from our kids emotionally.

"It is simply not prudent to write off a son or daughter, no matter how foolish, irritating, selfish, or insane a child may seem to be. You need to be there, not only while his or her canoe is bouncing precariously, but also after the river runs smooth again. You have the remainder of your life to reconstruct the relationship that is now in jeopardy. Don't let anger fester for too long. Make the first move toward reconciliation. And, finally, be respectful, even when punishment or restrictions are necessary. Then wait for the placid water in the early twenties."

—Dr. James Dobson in *The Complete Marriage and Family Home Reference Guide*

YOUR STORY
discovering where you stand

1. If you're currently raising a teen, can you remember the time when your child burst onto the "teen scene?"

2. Have you noticed a marked, sustained volatility since that time or has it been relatively smooth?

3. If you've experienced some struggles or confrontations, what have they generally been about? Would your teen agree or disagree?

4. If you don't have teens yet, what do you expect will be your biggest points of conflict? Why do you think this? How will you hope to handle them?

SCREEN TIME
discussing the video

1. In the teen years, the period of silence can last for . . .

2. Rebellious and destructive behavior is less likely to occur when . . .

3. Giving teens large quantities of unstructured time is . . .

4. The key to adolescent discipline (if one exists) is . . .

5. What teens need most from you as the parent is . . .

6. The four essentials to "making it through":
a.
b.
c.
d.

WORDWORKS
input from the Bible

1. "Every year his [Jesus'] parents went to Jerusalem for the Feast of the Passover. When he was twelve years old, they went up to the Feast, according to the custom. After the Feast was over, while his parents were returning home, the boy Jesus stayed behind in Jerusalem, but they were unaware of it. Thinking he was in their company,

they traveled on for a day. Then they began looking for him among their relatives and friends. When they did not find him, they went back to Jerusalem to look for him. After three days they found him in the temple courts, sitting among the teachers, listening to them and asking them questions. Everyone who heard him was amazed at his understanding and his answers. When his parents saw him, they were astonished. His mother said to him, 'Son, why have you treated us like this? Your father and I have been anxiously searching for you.'

"'Why were you searching for me?' he asked. 'Didn't you know I had to be in my Father's house?' But they did not understand what he was saying to them. Then he went down to Nazareth with them and was obedient to them" (Luke 2:41-51).

According to your answers about this passage last week, how would you say Jesus demonstrates the difference between strong will and defiance?

How do you think Jesus knew so well where He belonged at such a young age? Do you see evidence in your child of this kind of security, or could it be improved?

No doubt, like all adolescents, Jesus learned from His parents, even while teaching them good parenting. What are some lessons you've received from your son or daughter?

2. "He decreed statutes for Jacob and established the law in Israel, which he commanded our forefathers to teach their children, so the next generation would know them, even the children yet to be born, and they in turn would tell their children. Then they would put their trust in God and would not forget his deeds but would keep his commands" (Psalm 78:5-7).

When you think of how your child might influence future generations, how does it make you feel? Which aspects of your current relationship do you think will be most beneficial to your grandchildren? Why?

What attributes do you hope your child will carry on to your grandchildren?

What does this passage indicate as the key to ensuring children know God's works and respect His commands? Why is respect for God's law so important?

YOUR WAY
applying the
principles

1. Name one activity you think your (present or future) teen might enjoy taking up.

When you think of the current activities your teen is involved in, which is closest to your response?
___ "They're great!"
___ "I'm not sure."
___ "Some of her activities are good, others I don't know about."
___ "My kid has nothing going on."
___ (other) _____

2. If you have a teenager, think of a recent struggle between the two of you. If you don't have a teenager yet, use the following scenario: Your high schooler is set on attending a faraway university with a reputation as a "party school"; you want him or her to go to a nearby, small college that promotes Judeo-Christian values.

Now let's apply the three steps to coping with strong-willed teens to your situation. Describe as specifically as you can what you'd do as you follow the three steps.

Step 1: OFFER RESPECT AND DIGNITY
(Example: "Instead of talking down to him, I'd ask him to explain why he wants to go to that school.")

Step 2: VERBALIZE CONFLICTS AND RE-ESTABLISH BOUNDARIES

(Example: "I'd explain why the small college's values are important and how they're different from those of the university. I'd tell him that he's free to choose his school, but I'm free not to pay for a school I don't believe in.")

Step 3: LINK BEHAVIOR WITH CONSE-QUENCES

(Example: "I'd explain that if he refuses to choose a school I can support, he'll have to pay his own way. That may mean starting school a year late so that he can earn some money first.")

3. According to Dr. Dobson, the tools available to force compliance with teenagers are weak. What are some of the tools (keys to the car, the family purse, etc.) you have implemented to gain leverage with your teen recently? If you don't have a teen, which do you think you might favor?

4. Dr. Dobson recommends keeping a "reserve army" maintained rather than committing everything to the "busyness of living." If 10 is over-committed and 1 is not committed at all, circle the number where you see yourself on the continuum of that scale.

1   2   3   4   5   6   7   8   9   10

5. Dr. Dobson's 4 keys to getting through the turbulent years with your teen are, keep the schedule simple, get plenty of rest, eat nutritious meals, and stay on your knees. Which of these do you think is most important?

TECH SUPPORT
get your questions answered

Q. I thought the "twos" were terrible, but at least then I could physically restrain my child when he was defiant. Now that he's a teenager, he's taller and stronger than I am. He doesn't respond to my verbal reminders, either. What am I supposed to do?

A. One of the most common mistakes of parenthood is to be drawn into verbal battles with our children which leave us exhausted but without strategic advantage. Let me say it again: Don't yield to this impulse. Don't argue with your teen. Don't subject him to perpetual threats and finger-wagging accusations and insulting indictments. And most important, don't *nag* him endlessly. Adolescents hate to be nagged by "Mommy" and "Daddy"! When that occurs, they typically "protect" themselves by appearing deaf. Thus, the quickest way to terminate all communication between generations is to follow a young person around the house, repeating the same monotonous messages of disapproval with the regularity of a cuckoo clock. . . .

If yakety-yakking is not the answer, then what is the proper response to slovenliness, disobedience, defiance, and irresponsibility? That question takes us back to the threat to make a teen miserable if he doesn't cooperate. Don't let the news leak out, but the tools available to implement that promise are relatively weak. Since it is unwise (and unproductive) to spank a teenager, parents can only manipulate environmental circumstances (granting or withholding privileges, for example) when discipline is required. . . .

If policemen are unable to control teens today, then parents are in an even more delicate position. The early years of childhood are vital to the establishment of respect between generations. Without that foundation—without a touch of awe in the child's perception of his parent—then the balance of power and control is definitely shifted toward the younger combatant.

On the other hand, we must do the best job we can during the teen years, even if that foundation has not been laid. Parents must be willing to take whatever corrective action is required, but to avoid nagging, moaning, groaning, and growling when possible.

—Adapted from *The Strong-Willed Child*

CHAPTER 12

THE ULTIMATE PRIORITY

HOME BASE
getting started

After the middle adolescent age (ending at about fifteen years), children resent being told exactly what to believe. They don't want religion "forced down their throats," and should be given more autonomy in what they believe. . . . There is a brief period during childhood when youngsters are vulnerable to religious training. Their concepts of right and wrong are formulated during this time, and their view of God begins to solidify. . . . If the early exposure has been properly conducted, children will have an inner mainstay to steady them. Their early indoctrination, then, is the key to the spiritual attitudes they carry into adulthood.

—Dr. James Dobson in *The New Dare to Discipline*

YOUR STORY
discovering where you stand

1. What are your thoughts and feelings on the previous quote?

2. How would you compare your child's "spiritual age" (understanding of and commitment to God) with his chronological age? (For example, is he twelve years old but still praying the way he did when he was six?) How do you feel about that?

SCREEN TIME
discussing the video

1. Great personal sacrifice could be required to . . .

2. Protecting children is up to . . .

3. The ultimate priority is to . . .

Our love for Jesus

4. The window of opportunity for this to happen tends to be . . .

before 14

5. This generation doesn't know . . .

6. Erma Bombeck said raising kids is like . . .

WORDWORKS
input from
the Bible

1. "These commandments that I give you today are to be upon your hearts. Impress them on your children. Talk about them when you sit at home and when you walk along the road, when you lie down and when you get up. Tie them as symbols on your hands and bind them on your foreheads. Write them on the doorframes of your houses and on your gates." (Deuteronomy 6:6-9)

According to verse 6, who needs to learn God's commands?

What advice does this passage give on how to teach God's commands to children?

What would be the best places in your home to put Bible verses if you wanted your children to see them often?

2. "My son, do not forget my teaching, but keep my commands in your heart, for they will prolong your life many years and bring you prosperity. Let love and faithfulness never leave you; bind them around your neck, write them on the tablet of your heart. Then you will win favor and a good name in the sight of God and man. Trust in the LORD with all your heart and lean not on your own understanding; in all your ways acknowledge Him, and He will make your paths straight." (Proverbs 3:1-6)

According to Solomon, what will following his instruction give his son?

After listing these benefits, what is the first instruction Solomon gives?

Do your children understand the importance and benefits of trusting in the Lord? How do you know?

YOUR WAY
applying the
principles

1. Underline the statements you think your child could make at this point in life. Draw a box around those you think he or she couldn't truthfully make now, but that you'd like your child to be able to make someday.

"I pray on my own about things that matter to me."

"Church is boring."

"I have a personal relationship with Jesus."

"God made the world."

"Christians are hypocrites."

"I read the Bible on my own regularly."

"Jesus loves me."

"I do things to help people who have less than I do."

"I want to follow Jesus."

"I don't get anything out of Sunday school."

"I like going to church."

"I understand most of what I read in the Bible."

"Religion isn't a 'guy thing.'"

"My faith makes a difference in my decisions."

2. What are two or three of the statements above you'd like to see change? Commit to actively praying for those things over the next few weeks or months and also consider praying the prayer in the next section.

TECH SUPPORT
get your questions answered

"Most importantly, I urge you to hold your children before the Lord in fervent prayer day by day by day. Begin every morning with a prayer for wisdom and guidance. I am convinced that there is no other true source of confidence in parenting. There is not enough knowledge in the books, mine or anyone else's to counteract the evil that surrounds our kids today. We must bathe them in fervent prayer when we are in our prayer closet, saying words similar to these:

"Lord, You know my inadequacies. You know my weaknesses, not only in parenting, but in every area of my life. I'm doing the best I can to raise my kids properly, but it may not be good enough. As You provided the fish and the loaves to feed the five thousand hungry people, now take my meager effort and use it to bless my family. Make up for the things I do wrong. Satisfy the needs that I have not met. Compensate for my blunders and mistakes. Wrap Your great arms around my children, and draw them close to You. And be there when they stand at the great crossroads between right and wrong. All I can give them is my best, and I will continue to do that. I submit them to You now and rededicate myself to the task You have placed before me. The outcome rests securely in Your hands."

—From *The New Strong-Willed Child*

Wed, 4/10/2013

Where Do You Draw the line?

1. Bedtime
2. Homework
3. Sibling Communication
4. TV Time
   a) limits
   b) What to watch

5. Dating
6. Computers
7. Parent Child (Authority)
8. Reading Material
9. Outside Behavior
10. Dress

Review from Wed, 4/3/2010

- Discipline is what you do for a child

- Want to be good parents Love your wife

- Balance: Love & Control
- Parental leadership is God ordained

Tom & shelley Steck
TWS5@optimum.net

Video:

Irresponsibility .vs. Defiance
- Wilful Defiance Requires firm

Ultimate Paradox
- Parent have to earn the right to lead them

Six principles of earning the right to lead your child   pg. 18

1. Define boundaries in advance
2. Respond with confident Decisiveness
3. Distinguish between childhood irresponsibility .vs Defiance
4. Reassure & teach after confrontation
5. Avoid impossible demands

6. Let love be your guide

Disciplene ~ Building a lasting relationship through the years
For next wk Ch3 pg 27, 28, 29
   - your story
   - Word works
   - your way